A New Architecture for EU Gas Security of Supply

European Energy Studies

This series closely monitors the issues and developments in the field of European energy law and policy by providing an in-depth scholarly and research based yet a practical written and accessible source of information. The aim of this series is to publish up-to-date research for both practitioners and academics. It shall serve as comprehensible tool of knowledge offering detailed insight into the different pillars of EU energy policy tackling the underlying energy policies, legislation, energy economics and regulatory affairs, geopolitics and energy sources.

Volume 1
A New Architecture for EU Gas Security of Supply
Jean- Michel Glachant, Manfred Hafner, Jacques de Jong, Nicole Ahner, Simone Tagliapietra

Volume 2
EU Energy Innovation Policy Towards 2050
Jean-Michiel Glachant, Nicole Ahner and Leonardo Meeus

Volume 3
Sovereign Wealth Funds and Renewable Energy
Simone Tagliapietra

Volume 4
Security of Oil Supplies: Issues and Remedies
Giacomo Luciani

A New Architecture for EU Gas Security of Supply

Written by

Jean-Michel Glachant
Manfred Hafner
Jacques de Jong
Nicole Ahner
Simone Tagliapietra

CLAEYS & CASTEELS
2012

The deliberations at the four workshops greatly informed the views expressed in each chapter, but those views belong to the authors only and do not necessarily represent those of individual participants at the workshops or of the four supporting organisations.

ISBN 978 90 816 904 47

The paper and board used in the production of this book is sourced exclusively from replanted forests.

Published in 2012 by
Claeys & Casteels Publishing bv
Deventer (The Netherlands) – Leuven (Belgium)

P.O. Box 2013
7420 AA Deventer
The Netherlands
www.claeys-casteels.com

TABLE OF CONTENTS

Page

CHAPTER III THE BUILDING OF ENERGY SOLIDARITY IN THE EU

Nicole Ahner and Jean-Michel Glachant, Loyola de Palacio Chair, European University Institute

Foreword[1]

The European energy policy is very young and may be said to be still in its infancy. This may appear paradoxical when considering that the European Union started with two energy-driven Treaties in the Fifties: the European Coal and Steel Community in 1952 and the Euratom Treaty in 1957 gave always the impression that energy was a European affair. However, in spite of these two precedents demonstrating the importance attached by the six founding members of the Union to energy, it took more than another fifty years to see, with the adoption of the Lisbon Treaty, the introduction of a true Energy Title in the Treaty on the Functioning of the European Union (TFEU).

Article 194.1(b) of the TFEU provides that

"in the context of the establishment and functioning of the internal market and with regard to the need to preserve and improve the environment, Union policy on energy shall aim, in a spirit of solidarity between Member States, to ... (b) ensure security of energy supply in the Union."

This provision enshrines the first legal recognition of the concept of security of energy supply at European level and it came after numerous attempts to create a strong legal basis for the European energy policy. Up to then each Member State had considered that ensuring security of energy supply was a key component of its national sovereignty, a good reason to prevent the European Union to exert any competence in this sector. This had been recognised by the Court of Justice in a number of cases, e.g. to justify an exception to the free movement of goods. And indeed the whole structure of the energy sector in most Member States had been organised in such a way as to ensure the control of the State on the energy supply: vertically integrated state owned companies enjoying a supply monopoly of gas and electricity, regulated prices, numerous public service obligations, taxation of energy and bilateral intergovernmental agreements with key supplying third countries like Russia were the evidence

1 The views expressed by the author are his own and do not necessarily represent the position of the European Commission.

of the omnipotence of national authorities to deal with energy. Only the oil sector was escaping this national omnipresence, due to the control of the sector by vertically integrated international oil companies, being the owners of the oil reserves. But in this sector also the trend has now been reversed with the national oil companies controlling the resources.

This situation made the European Commission quite aware of the importance of security of supply and of the need to Europeanise the concept. It issued in November 2000 a Green paper on the security of energy supply, drawing attention to the structural weaknesses and geopolitical, social and environmental shortcomings of the European Union's energy supply. It put forward 13 questions to which thousands of answers have been received by the Commission in 2001. The need to develop a Europe-wide security of supply concept which alone will enable Europe to control its energy future was recognised by many respondents and the decade will see a rapid evolution towards such a concept, considerably helped by some significant Europe-wide disruption of electricity and gas supplies. From the major oil shock of 1973 and until 2000, European citizens were probably convinced that energy was plenty and that its supply was guaranteed. And Europe is probably the continent which has always enjoyed the best situation in this regard, compared with all other continents where supply disruptions are daily or at least part of the energy landscape, including in USA. But the first decade of the third millennium witnessed new worrying events in Europe reminding that security of supply is not guaranteed and that it should remain a key preoccupation of all Member States and of the European Union. Reference may be made here to the 2003 electricity black out in Italy originating in Switzerland, to the November 2006 blackout originating in Northern Germany and spreading throughout Western Europe up to Portugal; the January 2006 Russian gas supply through Ukraine disruption and a much worse repetition of it in January 2009, lasting two weeks in a rather cold winter but fortunately in the middle of an economic crisis which had reduced the gas demand.

Although a lot is still work in progress, in the last five years, the European Union, supported by all its Member States, has made huge progress towards a common energy policy, including a common concept of security of energy supply, the most sensitive issue for the Member States. This means that the Member States have now understood and agreed that, by acting more collectively, they may also improve their individual situation. This is fully in line with the principle of subsidiarity defined by Article 5.3 TFEU i.e. "the

Union shall act only if and in so far as the objectives of the proposed action cannot be sufficiently achieved by the Member States, either at central level or at regional and local level, but can rather, by reason of the scale or effects of the proposed action, be better achieved at Union level". No doubt that in the field of energy, EU action will be further needed.

Jean-Arnold Vinois
April 2012

The authors

Nicole Ahner is the scientific Coordinator of the Loyola de Palacio Chair at the European University Institute, Florence. Her research interests cover European law, energy and environmental law. Nicole studied law at the University of Bielefeld (Germany). There she graduated with the first State Law Exam [J.D. equivalent] in 2000, and obtained in 2002 the Second State Law Exam [bar exam equivalent]. Nicole defended her PhD at the University of Bielefeld in October 2007. She was visiting fellow at the European and Comparative Law Institute at the University of Oxford in 2007. In 2008 she was selected for a Jean Monnet Fellowship at the RSCAS (EUI). As of 2009 she has worked for Prof. Jean-Michel Glachant as a research assistant. Nicole has presented her research at international conferences and published academic articles on the topic of EU energy law, climate policy and international trade. Nicole joined the Florence School of Regulation in September 2009. She holds a PhD in Law from the University of Bielefeld. She also holds the degree of Master of Laws (LL.M.) in Legal Theory and European Law from the European Academy of Legal Theory in Brussels.

Jean-Michel Glachant is Holder of the Loyola de Palacio Chair and the Director of the Florence School of Regulation at the European University Institute, Florence. He is Professor in Economics and holds a PHD from La Sorbonne University, Paris. Jean-Michel is Member of the EU-Russia Gas Advisory Council of Commissioner Oettinger (EC), he is or has been advisor to DG TREN, DG COMP, DG RESEARCH and DG ENERGY of the European Commission and Coordinator / Scientific Advisor of several European research projects like THINK, SESSA, CESSA, Reliance, EU-DEEP, RefGov, TradeWind, Secure and Optimate. He is member of the Advisory Board of the E-Price project and Research Partner of CEEPR, (MIT – USA), EPRG (Cambridge University – UK), and Chief-Editor of "EEEP: Economics of Energy and Environmental Policy", a new journal of the International Association for Energy Economics.

Manfred Hafner is Professor in international relations and energy studies at the Johns Hopkins University (SAIS), at Sciences Po Paris School of International Affairs and at Skolkovo School of Management (BP Professor) in Moscow; he coordinates energy policy activities at the Fondazione Eni Enrico Mattei (FEEM) and is President for Europe, MENA, Russia and CIS at International Energy Consultants (IEC). He also teaches/taught at other prestigious universities among which are the Ecole des Mines de Paris, IFP-School, HEC-Paris, the Florence School of Regulation and the Geneva Graduate Institute of International and Development Studies. He has consulted extensively on energy issues for industry, governments and international organizations and was for many years the Scientific Director of the Observatoire Méditerranéen de l'Energie (OME). He is member of the EU-Russia Gas Advisory Council. Dr. Hafner holds master degrees in energy engineering, economics and policy from the Technische Universität München (Germany), the Institut Français du Pétrole (France), the Université Paris2/Panthéon Assas (France) and the University of Pennsylvania (USA) and a PhD from the Ecole des Mines de Paris.

Jacques de Jong is a Senior Fellow at the Cingendael International Energy Program (CIEP) since 2003. Before that he developed since 1971 a long experience in government energy policy making at the Dutch ministry of Economic Affairs. In various functions and responsibilities he worked on international oil policy issues (including the 1973 crisis and the set-up of the IEA), on electricity policy and more specific on nuclear and coal issues, on (national) energy market designs and energy utility structures, including policymaking on energy market liberalisation. In 1998 he became the first Dutch energy regulator, and started to play a key role in EU energy market issues, as a co-founder of the CEER (Council of European Energy Regulators) and in the Florence and Madrid Fora. As a CIEP-fellow he has published a number of papers and studies.

Simone Tagliapietra is Researcher at Fondazione Eni Enrico Mattei (FEEM), where he is involved in the "Energy: Resources and Markets" Research Programme. Prior to joining FEEM in March 2011, Simone completed a six-month internship at the Sustainable Energy Division of the United Nations Economic Commission for Europe (UNECE) in Geneva, Switzerland. His main areas of research are: European energy policy, security of energy supply, geopolitics of energy, gas markets analysis. Specifically, he is interested in the political and economic aspects of energy cooperation in the Euro-

Mediterranean region, with a particular concentration in the evolution of the regional gas market and the renewable energy potential in the Southern Mediterranean. Simone graduated in Political Science and International Relations from the Catholic University of Milan, with a thesis on the political economy of Sovereign Wealth Funds.

Introduction

Exploring the idea of a new EU gas security of supply architecture requires some further reflection on the concept of energy supply security. Many definitions are used and many approaches are defined when energy supply security is at stake. Energy availability, continuity of energy supplies and price-affordability are some of the notions that are used, with all their different connotations. Some of the security arguments are rational, but it cannot be denied that also quite some irrational and even emotional arguments are used. In some regions and policy-circles for instance, energy security is largely focusing on oil supply from the Middle East, whereas elsewhere it is basically about gas from Russia. In the EU policy arena all these elements are heard and the policy approach that is developed is somewhat diffused and has therefore various degrees of public and political backing.

When the security of supply concept is further analysed, a number of different aspects and (pre-) conditions could be mentioned and could be further used. Would for instance an integrated energy approach be the preferred route, or should the focus be on a specific fuel. This could be done when there are no direct fuel alternatives at stake. Another issue could be the choice between focusing on securing the supply of energy commodities, and hence a further discussion on the role of markets and/or contracts. But as relevant could be the discussion on system adequacy and system reliability. Most fuels travel through the value chains and require various degrees of transformation and transmission before energy consumers are served. Security of supply could therefore be very much dependent on the adequacy and the reliability of the systems that are needed. A further aspect might be the policy question to set quantitative or qualitative objectives in the choice for supplies and suppliers? Timing is then also issue, as long term security assurances with a specific group of (external) suppliers could require the development of building supplier-consumer confidence. But when unforeseen and sudden interruptions of supply are taking place, different policy approaches are needed including short term emergency and/or solidarity arrangements.

The academic literature is rich with a variety of models, approaches, schemes covering almost all of the issues mentioned that could be considered relevant in the supply security concept. A 2010 OECD- study [2] gives an interesting and useful overview of the academic debate to date, with a number of quantitative examples. Mentioning one of them is the simplified version of a CIEP-ECN model for an integrated Supply/Demand Index. This index could be a useful one for further consideration in the EU as a policy tool for assessing and reviewing the supply security context of national and European energy policies. As an example figure 1 plots the application of the SSDI on an *ex post* and an *ex ante* basis on a scale from 0 to 100, with the higher the outcome the more secure the energy supply basis.

Figure 3.7: OECD countries with high values or increases in the SSDI between 1970 and 2007

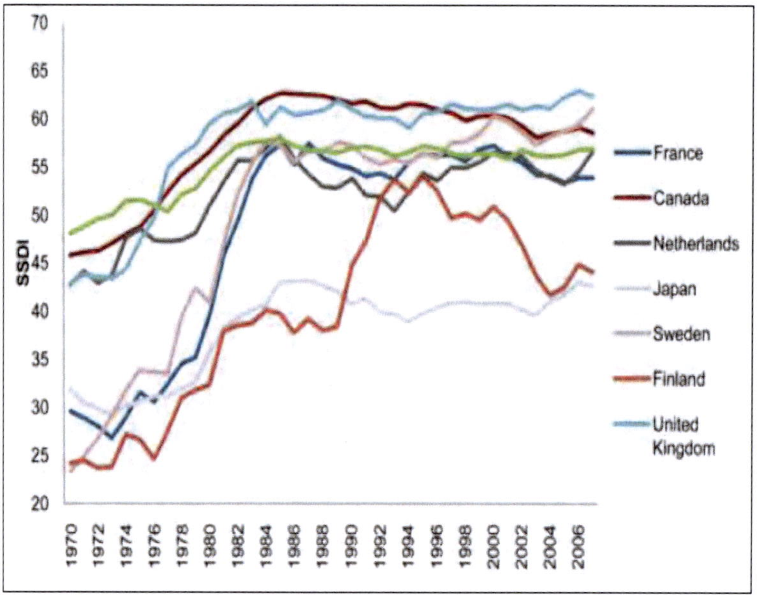

Source: The Security of Energy Supply and the Contribution of Nuclear Energy; OECD 2010

2 Reference: The Security of Energy Supply and the Contribution of Nuclear Energy; OECD 2010, ISBN 978-92-64-09634-9

Figure 2.14: The S/D Index of EU Member States in 2020

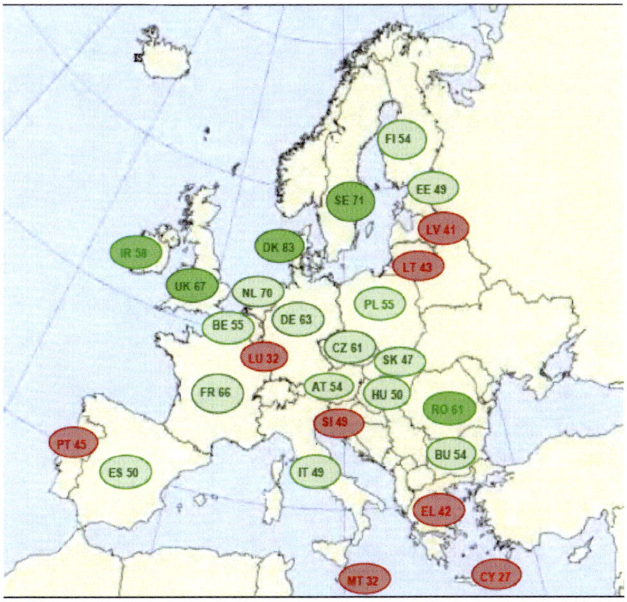

Source: The Security of Energy Supply and the Contribution of Nuclear Energy; OECD 2010

Considering the discussion on the supply security concept and further reflecting on the idea of a new architecture for the EU's gas supply security, the following notions are coming to mind:

- A gas-specific quantified target for supply security may not be the right policy path to follow, as a more integrated approach for the energy fuel mix might be more appropriate.
- In the supply-demand equations, it could be useful to articulate more precisely the role of gas in the longer term fuel mix (destination, transition, consequence).
- All scenario's and forecasts of the role of gas lead to increasing roles for imports, hence requiring specific focus on the role of external gas suppliers for EU markets
- Building global confidence between consumers and suppliers could be considered as an essential element in a supply security architecture for gas.
- A distinction might usefully be made between the medium term (2020) and the longer term (2050), as existing EU policies are already focusing on 2020, whereas policies focusing on the roads towards 2050 are starting a process of reflection and discussion.

- The role of markets and infrastructures are essential elements in any type of Architecture for the EU's gas supply security.

A number of these reflections have found their way in the four workshop discussions that were held under the project and are further reported in the chapters of this book.

Jacques de Jong
Clingendael International Energy Programme, The Hague, Netherlands
March 2012

Clingendael International Energy Programme

The Clingendael International Energy Programme (CIEP) is an independent policy think-tank in the Netherlands, dealing with international energy policy developments and is well positioned to discuss energy issues in the geopolitical and wider political context. Through research, the publication of studies and position papers, through the organisation of courses and training programmes, CIEP makes a fundamental contribution to the national and international public debate and policy agenda's on international politics and economic developments in the energy sector. CIEP's current activities revolve around the issue of the growing mismatch between long-term energy needs, climate change visions and short-term market developments. It focuses on subject areas such as the development of European Energy Markets, the wider international economic and geopolitical aspects of the oil and gas markets and the issues around energy and sustainable development, with its focus on transition towards and governance structures of decarbonised energy markets.

To know about the activities of CIEP visit www.clingendael.nl/ciep

Fondazione Eni Enrico Mattei

Fondazione Eni Enrico Mattei (FEEM) is a nonprofit, nonpartisan research institution devoted to the study of sustainable development and global governance. Officially recognized by the President of the Italian Republic in 1989 and in full operation since 1990, FEEM has grown to become a leading research centre, providing timely and objective analysis on a wide range of environmental, energy and global economic issues. FEEM's mission is to improve through research the quality of decision-making in public and private spheres. This goal is achieved by creating an international and multidisciplinary network of researchers working on several innovative programmes, by providing and promoting training in specialized areas of research, by disseminating research results through a wide range of outreach activities, and by delivering directly to policy makers via participation in various institutional fora.

To know about the activities of FEEM visit www.feem.it

The Loyola de Palacio Chair

The Loyola de Palacio Chair has been created in honour of the former Vice-President of the Commission and Commissioner for Energy and Transport (1999-2004) Loyola de Palacio (1950-2006). The Chair hosted by the European University Institute within its Robert Schuman Centre of Advanced Studies conducts advanced research beyond disciplinary boundaries on feasible proposals for EU energy policy. Bringing together academics in the fields of law, economics and engineering it offers cross-disciplinary alliances and a platform for innovative thinking, dialogue and networking between academics, practitioners and decision-makers to define and propose feasible evolutions of EU energy governance.

To know about the activities of the Chair visit www.loyola-de-Palacio-Chair.eu

Wilton Park

Wilton Park is a global forum for strategic discussion organising over 50 events a year in the UK and overseas, bringing together leading representatives from the worlds of politics, business, academia, diplomacy, civil society and media. We focus on issues of international security, prosperity and justice. Our meetings provide a neutral environment where conflicting views can be expressed and debated openly and calmly, allowing acceptable compromise and resolution to be achieved. We encourage innovation in global thinking by provoking lively debate and promote inclusivity among the policy-makers and opinion formers. Discussions are non-attributable to encourage frank exchanges and open dialogue."

To know about the activities of Wilton Park visit http://www.wiltonpark.org.uk/en/

CHAPTER I

EU EXTERNAL RELATIONS AND ITS RELATION TO GAS INFRASTRUCTURE

Manfred Hafner, Fellow, Fondazione Eni Enrico Mattei (FEEM)
Simone Tagliapietra, Researcher, Fondazione Eni Enrico Mattei (FEEM)

1. Security of supply and security of demand: two sides of the same coin

Energy security has two mutually supportive sides: security of supply and security of demand. One cannot exist without the other. This is a fundamental element that the EU, which has traditionally paid more attention to security of supply, should always take into consideration. The European gas industry has experienced an extraordinary success over the last decades. A strongly interconnected network of gas pipelines has been developed inside Europe and between Europe and its gas suppliers (both by pipeline and Liquefied Natural Gas (LNG)). However, the European energy industry is today facing huge and unprecedented uncertainties. Major open questions are: (i) Will Europe comply with its 20-20-20 targets on renewable energy, energy efficiency and greenhouse gas (GHG) emissions? (ii) How seriously will Europe (and the world) pursue and implement climate change policies towards a low carbon economy? (iii) What will EU national nuclear policies be in a post-Fukushima world? (iv) Will large-scale availability of Carbon Capture and Storage (CCS) allow the re-launch of clean coal and allow widespread use of natural gas after 2025? (v) Will the North American exploitation of unconventional gas be reproducible in other parts of the world? (vi) Will necessary upstream and midstream investments be carried out in due time? (vii) What will be the position of major suppliers such as Norway, the Middle East and North Africa (MENA), the Caspian Basin and Russia? (viii) What will be the effect of the recent Arab uprisings on MENA gas supplies?

The gas market has dramatically changed over the last few years. The supply balance for Europe and the rest of the world has switched from tight to loose. The discussion has also shifted from questions such as "how to secure long or short-term contracts?", to "where should all the contracted gas go?". It could be that the pendulum is already swinging back and that in a few years we will again face a tight market. The reason for these cycles, where the market goes from a situation of undersupply to oversupply and back to undersupply and so on, is due to the long lead times of developing new gas supply infrastructure which cannot react quickly to changes in demand.

The energy system and therefore the gas industry are not isolated from what happens in the rest of the economy. The global financial crisis and the following economic recession have caused major confusion in energy and gas markets around the world. While gas demand declined in the wake of the economic downturn, new supply surged mainly because of the increase in global LNG supply and the so-called shale gas revolution in North America. This unprecedented shift in supply-demand balances created new dynamics in the European gas industry and strongly put into question established gas price formation mechanisms. The important difference between oil price indexed gas prices (mainly present on the European continent) and hub based gas prices created tensions between the EU and some of its major gas suppliers.

2. European natural gas demand

European domestic gas production has inexorably fallen over the last decades (from 232 bcm in 2000 to 175 bcm in 2010), while natural gas demand has gradually increased. Demand grew on average by 4,2 % during the 1990s, and by 2% from 2000 to 2008. European gas demand strongly decreased in 2009 for the first time, primarily because of global financial turmoil. In 2010, the level of European gas demand bounced back, reaching a new all-time high of 493 bcm[3], mainly because of a slight economic recovery and a cold winter. The first data available for 2011 estimated a new decrease in gas demand, due to the worsening of the economic crisis and a mild winter.

3 Unless otherwise stated, all gas statistics in this chapter refer to the BP Statistical Review.

Gas demand in the EU-27 member states (1965-2011)

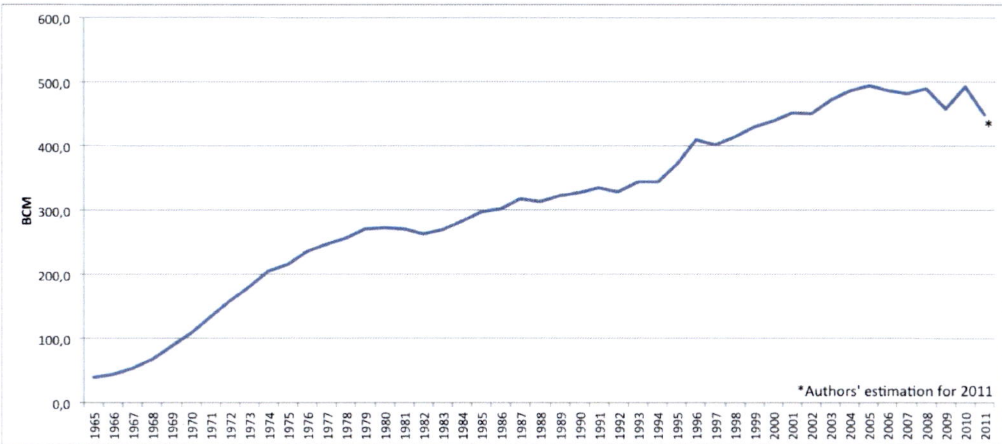

Data source: BP Statistical Review (June 2011)

In 2010 the EU imported natural gas mainly from Russia (110 bcm), Norway (99 bcm), Algeria (50 bcm) and Qatar (34 bcm) followed by smaller suppliers such as Nigeria (15 bcm), Libya (10 bcm), Trinidad and Tobago (6 bcm), Egypt (4 bcm). The EU dependency on external suppliers, represented by the imports/consumption ratio, stood at 67% in 2010.

EU gas supply – 2010 (and % of imports)

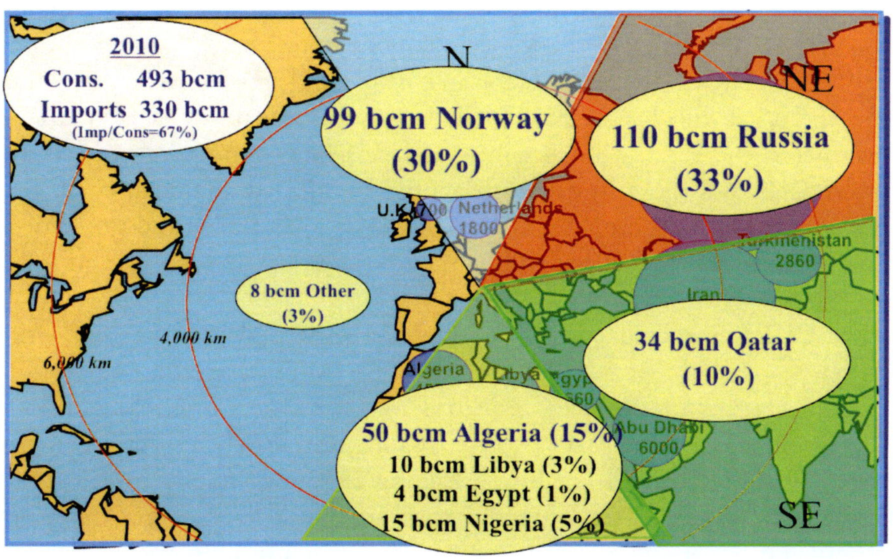

Data source: BP Statistical Review (June 2011)

Looking at the variety of projections on future EU-27 gas demand made by different institutions, it is possible to demonstrate the high level of uncertainty. Some projections (mainly industry based) show an increasing gas demand, while others (integrating strong climate policies) show a declining gas demand.

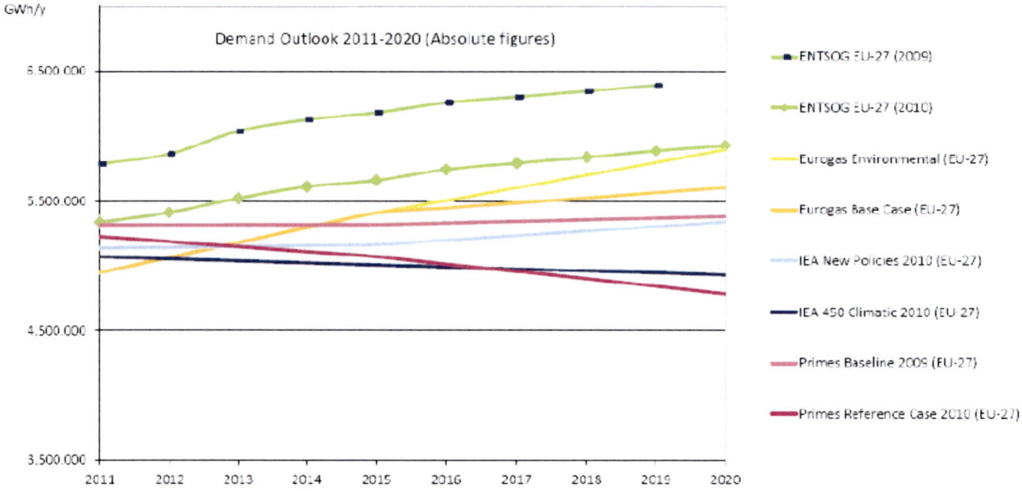

Source: ENTSOG TYNDP

The EU's import needs in the long-term remain a major question mark. This general uncertainty is not only due to the great uncertainty of EU gas demand, but also to uncertainties in EU domestic supply. In this sense, major questions are: how quickly will the European – in particular UK – domestic gas supply decrease? What will be the role of shale gas in some European countries? Nevertheless the greatest uncertainty, as far as long-term gas prospects are concerned, relates more to demand security than to supply security. In this sense, major questions are: How seriously will Europe pursue and implement climate change policies? What will be the role of gas in this context?

2.1 SECURE Scenarios

SECURE (*Security of Energy Considering its Uncertainty, Risk and Economic implications*) was a three-year (2008-2010) major research project on energy security of supply carried out by 15 leading European research institutions (FEEM was the scientific coordinator) and funded by the European Commission under the Seventh Framework Programme. In the framework of this project a certain number of energy scenarios have been produced. In fact, between now and 2050, mankind must face two intertwined problems: the growing scarcity of oil (and to some respect gas, but not of coal) and the accumulation of GHG in the atmosphere. These "bathtub problems" cannot be considered independently, as hydrocarbon scarcity paves the way to coal (and hence higher GHG emissions) while climate policies open the path to low carbon societies. "Smart" energy policies and associated international relations should combine the security, the sustainability as well as the competitiveness dimensions. A family of scenarios has been developed in the SECURE project using the POLES model to illustrate the complex interactions of climate policies and energy security issues:

- The Muddling Through (MT) scenario describes the consequences of non-coordinated, low profile climate policies;
- The Europe Alone case (EA) represents the outcome of a scenario in which every country is free-riding except the EU;
- The Global Regime (GR) explores a new energy system, under strong emission constraint (EU-type). The two latter scenarios imply a new energy paradigm for the EU.

Scenarios with limited and uncoordinated action for reducing GHGs emissions, such as Muddling Through imply only weak signals in terms of carbon price. As they mobilize the cheap part of the Marginal Abatement Cost curves, they already change significantly the level of emissions through reduced demand, accelerated development of non-fossil energy (both nuclear and renewables) and CCS. However, these scenarios do not succeed in meeting the emission targets deemed desirable in the latest IPCC Assessment Report in order to limit average temperature increase to 2°C above pre-industrial levels.

Scenarios with strong climate policies, such as Global Regime, clearly allow reducing both emissions and the level of tension on international hydrocarbon markets, through lower oil and gas production. This is a double dividend situation, probably the most important one to be derived from ambitious climate policies.

Finally, scenarios with unilateral actions from Europe involving a change of paradigm for the European energy system (in Europe alone) do not meet the climate target as the impacts of efforts in Europe are not sufficient to induce massive emission reductions at world level, nor do they limit the risk of energy shocks. However, these scenarios have highly beneficial implications for Europe.

A thorough restructuring of the European energy system results from domestically imposing strong emission reduction. This restructuring improves resilience to energy shocks and allows Europe to be protected by lower energy demand, higher contribution of domestic non-fossil fuels (renewable and nuclear) and a much lower level of fossil fuel imports. On the other hand this scenario implies important transition costs for the EU.

Scenarios that involve no drastic change in Europe's energy system imply the development of the energy security strategy in a conventional setting: the main concern is to ensure that sufficient supply is available, particularly of oil and gas supply. The European Energy Charter that currently provides the basis for this policy is just one of the possible options. The key issue is the possibility of a timely investment for the development of huge production and transport capacities. In that case the Energy Charter should at least be completed by other policies.

One of the permanent requests of exporting countries is for the importers to ensure the demand security that will guarantee the cost-effectiveness of the supply and transport investments. They also call for the possibility of downstream investment. This type of policy framework would result in some upstream-downstream reintegration of the industries, with cross investments in common projects or joint ventures. Based more on bilateral relationships this type of policy may, however, enter into contradiction with the liberalization and Energy Charter perspectives.

Scenarios that imply a deep restructuring of the European energy sector and energy demand change the market perspectives for the exporters. Demand, when impacted by strong environmental constraints in Europe will display very different dynamics, in particular after 2030. If Europe is alone in its efforts to develop a new energy paradigm (eg Europe Alone scenario) the effectiveness in terms of climate change mitigation policies and even the impact on global energy markets will be limited given the moderate weight of the EU on a global scale; however Europe will be less vulnerable to energy shocks. If some kind of global climate regime is implemented, then energy will be more sustainable in the long term, but in the short term there is a risk of producing countries underinvesting because of the uncertainties created.

This case would provide a very challenging setting for the development of cooperative relations between importer countries and their suppliers. New orientations may encompass economic collaborations on new low carbon technologies or reinforced economic cooperation in areas other than energy. Scenarios with a new energy paradigm display a lower demand and higher share of non-fossil domestic sources, whether renewable or nuclear. Primary energy demand for oil and coal drops, while gas demand is much less affected. Total electricity production is almost unchanged in the new paradigm scenarios because electricity is the main carrier of decarbonisation. Moreover the role of renewable, nuclear and CCS increases with the strengthening of the carbon constraint. Wind and biomass play the major role in the increase of the renewable power plant capacity in Europe.

In the Global Regime scenario, climate policies bring about a significant double dividend in terms of reduced tensions on energy markets and in terms of increased environmental sustainability. However the Global Regime scenario is highly sensitive to shocks in form of a very severe nuclear accident and/or failure to implement carbon capture and storage on a large scale. This underlines the need of stringent application of high-level safety standards for nuclear worldwide and intensification of efforts to develop and implement CCS-systems. Overall it can be said that there are clear synergies between protection of climate and security of supply. Meeting ambitious GHG-emission reduction goals is also beneficial for security of supply, by means of successful decarbonisation of the energy supply system through expansion of renewables, nuclear and CCS, combined with very extensive efficiency improvements.

International energy prices in alternative SECURE scenarios

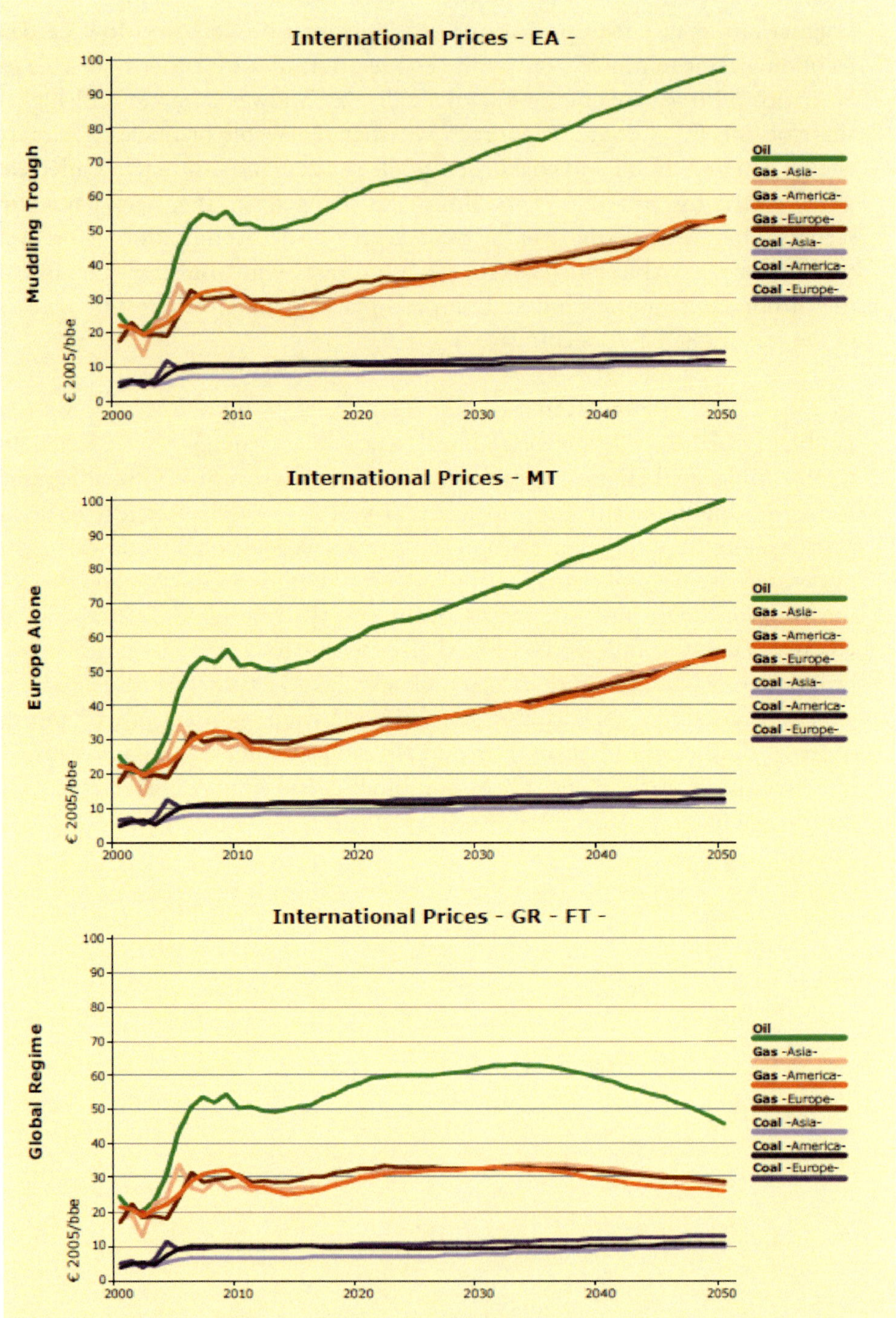

Prices in constant (2005) US dollars, per barrel of oil equivalent

Composition of energy primary consumption in the EU in alternative SECURE scenarios

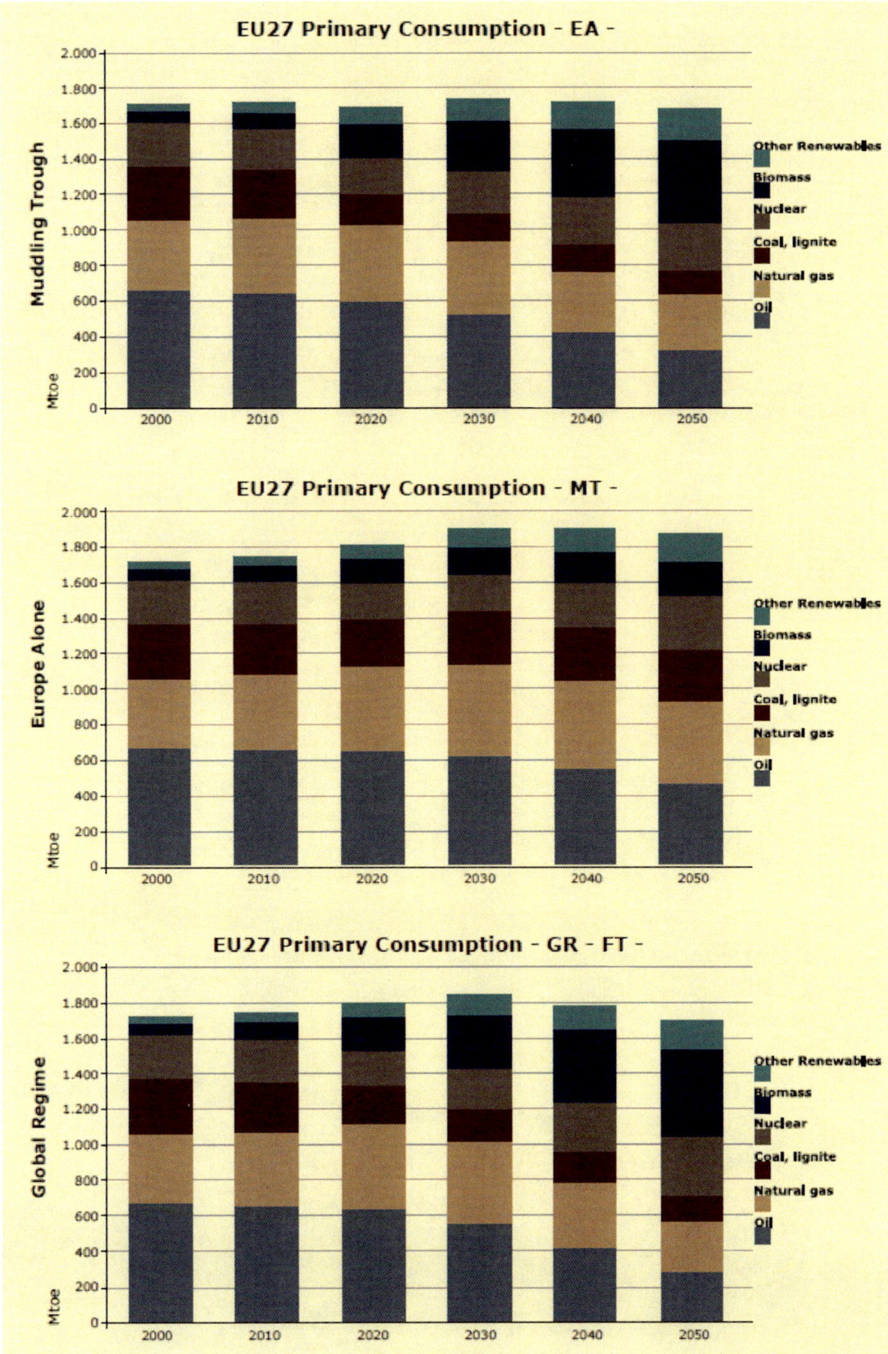

Millions of tons of oil equivalent

Electricity generation in the EU by technology -with and without CCS- in SECURE scenarios

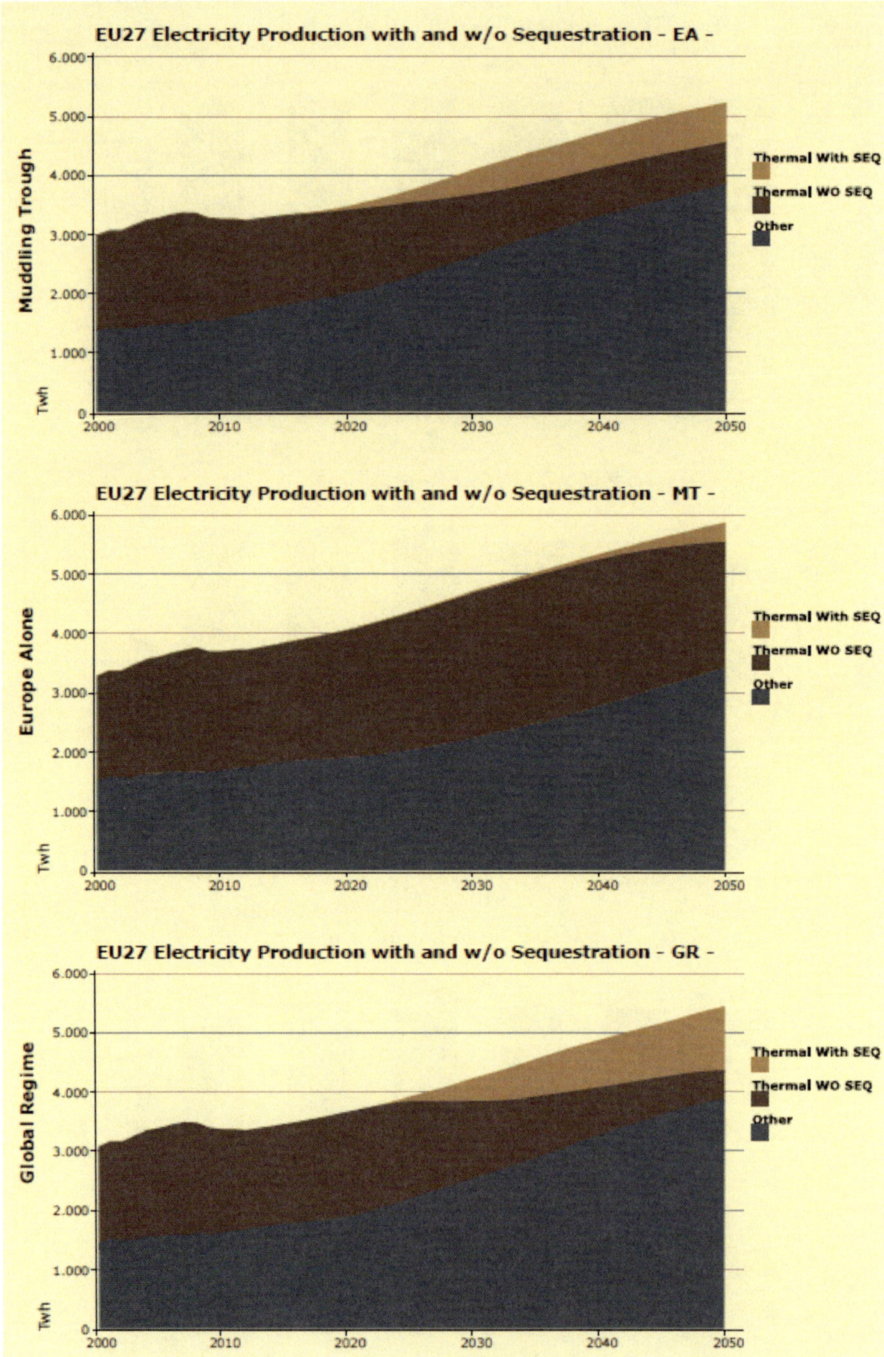

2.2 International Energy Agency scenarios

The International Energy Agency (IEA) highlighted on its World Energy Outlook 2011 (WEO-2011) the increasingly important role that natural gas is expected to play in the world energy mix. The WEO-2011 provides three scenarios: (i) The Current Policies Scenario, which takes account only of policies already formally adopted and implemented; (ii) The New Policies Scenario, which takes into account of recently announced commitments and plans even if they are yet to be formally adopted and implemented; (iii) The 450 Scenario, a pathway consistent with a 50% chance of meeting the goal of limiting the increase in average global temperature to 2°C). In all three scenarios, world natural gas demand is set to rise -by 2035- to a level even higher than previously projected, reflecting the impact of the 12th Five-Year Plan announced by China in 2011 (which envisages a major expansion of domestic use of natural gas), and the consequences of the damage to the Fukushima nuclear plant in Japan, which also contributed to push up projections of future gas consumption.

The WEO-2011 Current Policies Scenario takes account only of policies already formally adopted and implemented; the New Policies Scenario takes into account of recently announced commitments and plans even if they are yet to be formally adopted and implemented; the 450 Scenario is a pathway consistent with a 50% chance of meeting the goal of limiting the increase in average global temperature to 2°C). In the New Policies Scenario (the central scenario in the WEO-2011) the global demand for natural gas grows from 3.1 tcm in 2009 to 4.75 tcm in 2035, representing an average annual increase of 1.7% with the share of gas in the global energy mix rising from 21% in 2009 to 23% in 2035. Natural gas demand grows even more quickly in the Current Policies Scenario -at an average of 1.9% per year- to reach almost 5.1 tcm in 2035, while it slows down in the 450 Scenario -at an average of 0.9% per year- to tail off after 2030 as the market penetration of renewables increases.

World primary natural gas demand by scenario

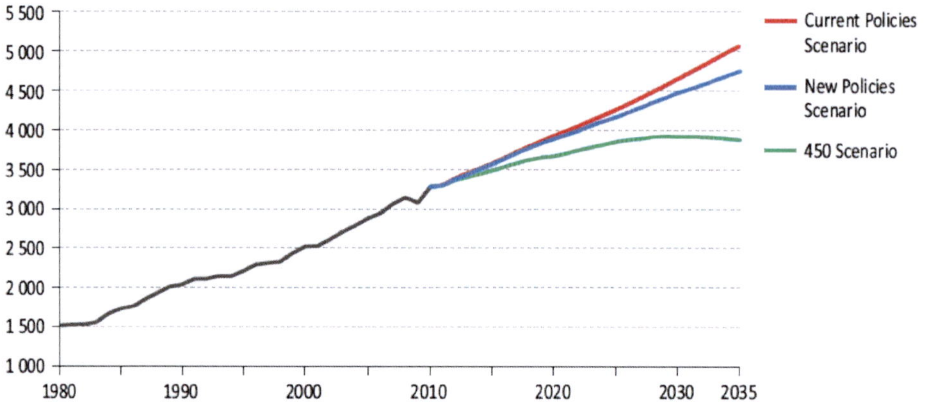

Source: IEA World Energy Outlook 2011

The IEA argues that in OECD countries, gas for the power sector accounts for the largest share of demand growth by 2035 (with the share of gas in the OECD electricity mix forecasted to rise up to 24% by 2035). This growing importance of natural gas in the OECD power generation sector is mainly due to policy choices (including carbon pricing in Europe); to the addition of more variable renewable energy sources; and it requires lower capital costs and shorter construction times than the main alternatives.

Natural gas demand by selected region in the IEA New Policies Scenario (2009 – 2035)

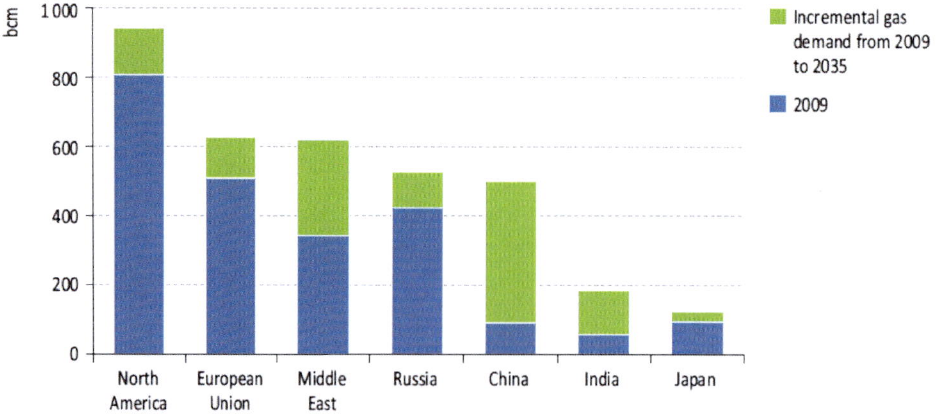

Source: IEA, World Energy Outlook 2011

According to the IEA New Policies Scenario, consumption of natural gas in the EU increases by an average of 0.8% per year from 2009 to 2035 to reach 615 bcm in 2035. In the Current Policies scenario gas demand would increase on average by 1.2% per year to 566 bcm while in the 450 Scenario it would decline on average by 0.5% per year to reach 367 bcm in 2035. In the power generation sector, gas demand increases between 2009 and 2035 on average by 1,3%/y in the New Policies Scenario, by 1.9%/y in the Current Policies scenario, and decreases by 2.1%/y in the 450. The underlying policy assumptions for the EU of the three IEA scenarios are as follows: The Current Policy Scenario integrates full implementation of the Emission Trading Scheme (ETS) covering power, industry and aviation, and full implementation of the building energy performance directive as well as implementation of emission standards for cars. This scenario is also based on a 20% reduction in emissions by 2020 compared with 1990 and a 20% share of renewables in energy demand in 2020. The New Policy Scenario for the EU assumes new and more stringent emission standards for trucks and cars. Finally, the 450 Scenario assumes a 30% reduction in emissions by 2020 compared with 1990 and a strengthened ETS in line with the Energy Roadmap 2050 (see below).

2.3 DG Climate: 2050 low carbon economy roadmap

Following the European Council's target to reduce GHG emissions by 80% to 95% below 1990 levels by 2050, the European Commission published in early 2011 a low carbon economy roadmap, elaborated by DG Climate. The next figure illustrates the most cost-effective pathway, according to DG Climate, to achieve the desired goal. As can be seen, the power generation and residential sectors – two traditional markets for gas demand – are expected to be almost fully decarbonised by 2050. Unless Carbon Capture and Storage (CCS) is heavily applied, the use of natural gas – which has the lowest climate impact of all fossil fuels – will need to be severely reduced. CCS is a technology that still needs to prove its widespread implementation and diffusion.

Optimal pathway to reduce GHG emissions by 80% in 2050

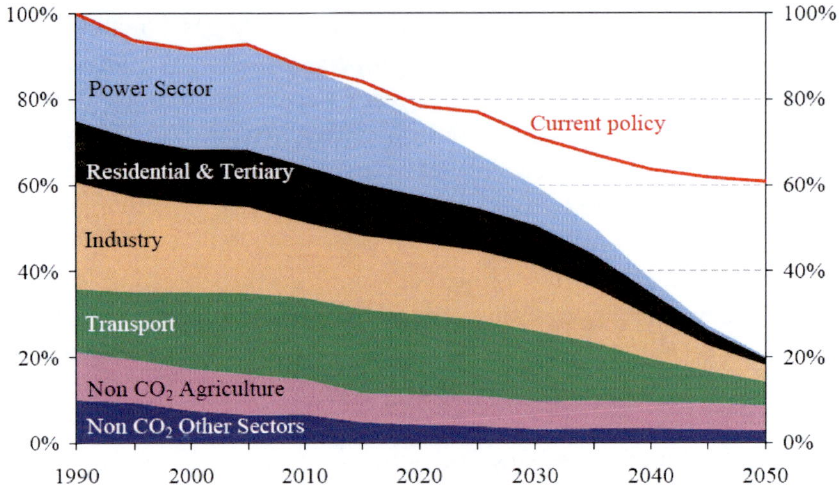

Source: European Commission – DG Climate

The DG Climate Low Carbon Economy roadmap and its impact to the energy sector was mainly a modeling exercise. The energy policy implications have been addressed by the Energy Roadmap published by DG Energy at the end of 2011.

2.4 DG Energy: Energy Roadmap 2050

On December 15, 2011, responding to a request advanced by the European Council held on February 4, 2011 the European Commission has adopted its Energy Roadmap 2050 elaborated by DG Energy, which explores the challenges posed by delivering the EU decarbonisation objective of reducing GHG emissions to 80-95% below 1990 levels by 2050, ensuring at the same time security of energy supply and competitiveness. Recognizing that today there is inadequate direction as to what should follow the EU 2020 agenda, the Energy Roadmap 2050 explores a number of scenarios to achieve an 80% reduction in GHG emissions (implying some 85% decline of energy-related CO2 emissions) by 2050, which suggest that a decarbonisation of the energy system is possible and can even be less costly than current policies in the long-run.

The European Commission also carried out an impact assessment at the basis of the Energy Roadmap 2050 to examine a set of possible future developments to get more robust information on how the energy system could achieve the decarbonisation target by 2050 and improve security of supply and competitiveness, without selecting one of them. For this, the European Commission identified four main decarbonisation routes for the energy sector – energy efficiency impacting mostly on the demand side and RES, nuclear and CCS predominantly on the supply side (lowering the carbon intensity of supply). The policy options (scenarios) proposed in the Energy Roadmap 2050 explore 5 different combinations of the four decarbonisation options. All decarbonisation scenarios achieve 85% energy related CO_2 emissions by 2050 and the impact assessment evaluates whether each policy option also improves security of supply and competitiveness of the energy sector as well as lead to affordable energy costs.

Policy options (scenarios) in the Energy Roadmap 2050

1	**Business as usual (Common Reference scenario)**
1bis	**Current Policy Initiatives – CPI scenario (updated Reference scenario)**
2	**High Energy efficiency scenario**
3	**Diversified supply technologies scenario**
4	**High RES scenario**
5	**Delayed CCS scenario**
6	**Low nuclear scenario**

Source: European Commission

As regards environmental impacts, all policy options significantly reduce energy consumption with the largest reduction coming in the "High Efficiency scenario". The composition of energy mix also differs significantly in a decarbonised system with strong increase in RES in all scenarios. Nuclear developments depend on policy assumptions taken and ranges from 2 to 18%. The share of gas is the highest in the "Low nuclear scenario" with significant CCS penetration. Electricity share in final energy consumption doubles from current levels.

According to the EC impact assessment, these various analyses of carbon and energy policies on GDP suggest that impact is rather limited. As regards electricity prices, some policy options show a small decrease in prices as compared to Reference or CPI scenarios ("Energy Efficiency" and "Diversified supply technologies") while some others show increases ("High RES" and to a lower extent "Low nuclear"). ETS prices are significantly higher than in the Reference and CPI scenarios, while fuel prices are lower. The Impact Assessment concludes that there is no clear winner among policy options scoring the best in all criteria and several trade-offs will need to be taken into account.
As far as European natural gas consumption is concerned, it falls substantially in all scenarios. Falls are greatest in decarbonisation scenarios, and especially in the "high renewables scenario", also if only after 2030. According to the decarbonisation scenarios of the Roadmap, EU gas consumption will reach a level of 348-384 mtoe in 2030 and nearby 210-295 mtoe in 2050 (compared with 437-443 mtoe in 2010).

Energy Roadmap 2050 scenarios: EU gas consumption (Mtoe)

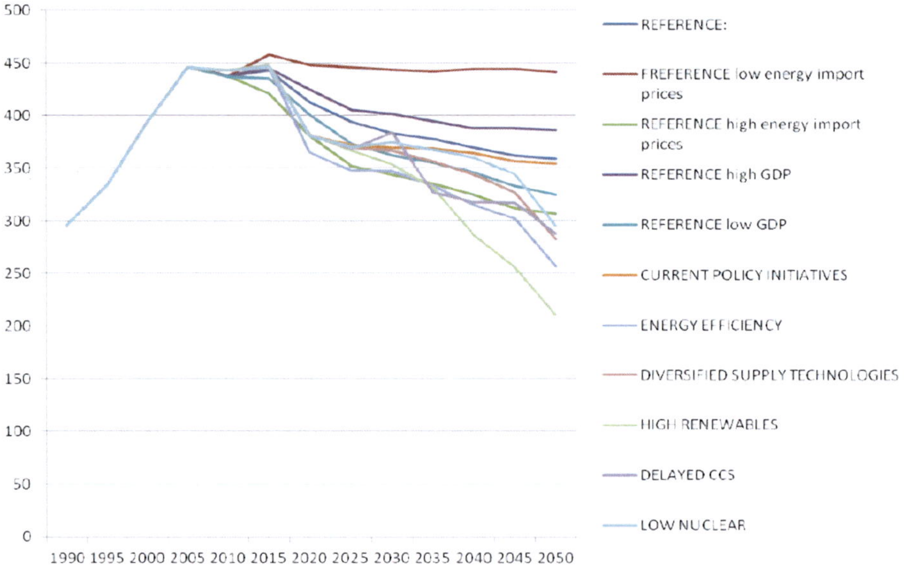

Source: Jonathan Stern (OIES) based on: European Commission, Energy Roadmap 2050

The Energy Roadmap 2050 underlines that natural gas will be critical for the transformation of the energy system, foreseeing that medium-term European gas demand will stay high especially in the power generation sector.

Energy Roadmap 2050 scenarios: gas input to power generation (Mtoe)

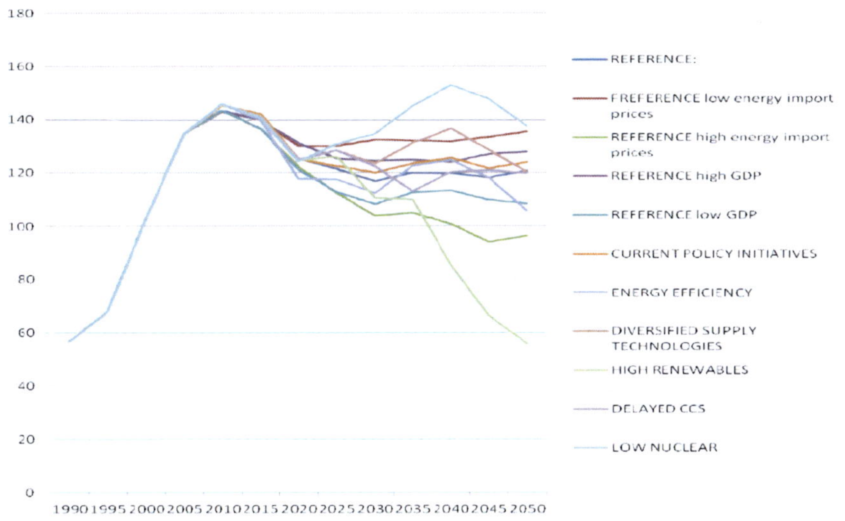

Source: Jonathan Stern (OIES) based on: European Commission, Energy Roadmap 2050

In fact, gas demand in power generation is relatively resilient (10-15% below 2010 levels in 2030), especially in the case of low nuclear where, after dipping, it increases during 2020-40. The worst case scenarios for gas are "High Renewables" and "High energy import prices", others are relatively stable until after 2040. The Energy Roadmap 2050 also considers that future developments of new potential supplies from unconventional gas sources in or around Europe and further internal market integration could decrease concerns on EU gas import dependency. However, in most scenarios European gas imports remain approximately at 2010 levels throughout the projected period, but imports fall significantly after 2035 in the majority of the decarbonisation scenarios.

Energy Roadmap 2050 scenarios: net gas imports (Mtoe)

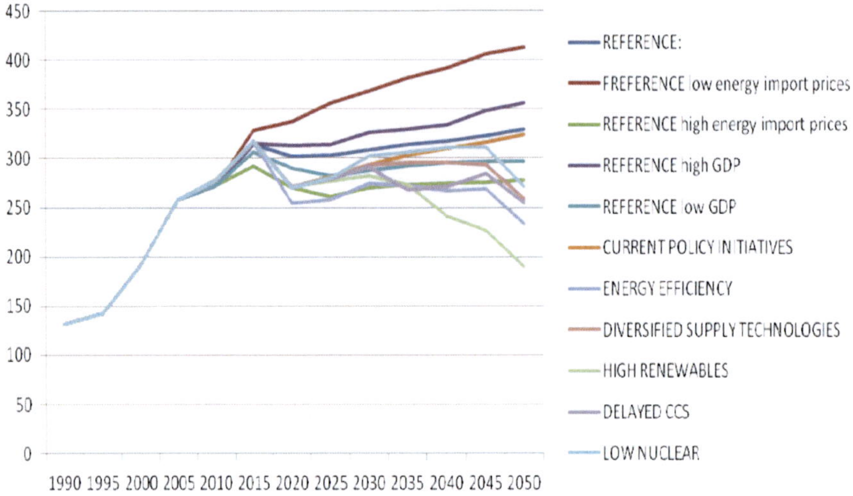

Source: Jonathan Stern (OIES) based on: European Commission, Energy Roadmap 2050

In the majority of the reference/current policies scenarios, import levels are similar to/above 2010 levels throughout the projection period, with the exception of "low energy import prices" where imports increase significantly. In the majority of the decarbonisation scenarios, imports remain roughly at 2010 levels for a significant part of the projection period falling significantly only after 2035. After 2035, the worst scenarios for gas are "high renewables" and (to a less extent) "energy efficiency".

Compared to other fossil fuels gas will perform much better and keep its 2005 share in primary energy consumption up to 2050 about constant in all decarbonization scenarios.

EU decarbonization scenarios – 2030 and 2030 range of fuel shares in primary energy consumption compared with 2005 outcome (in %)

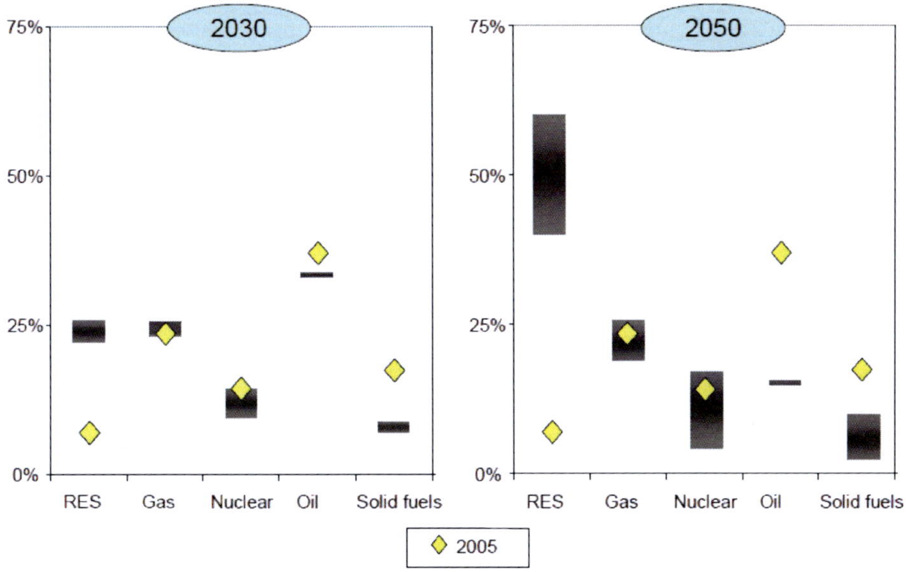

Source: European Commission

Concerning natural gas, the Roadmap affirms that gas will be critical for the transformation of the energy system. Substitution of coal (and oil) with gas in the short to medium term could help to reduce emissions with existing technologies until at least 2030 or 2035. Although gas demand in the residential sector might drop by a quarter until 2030 due to several energy efficiency measures in the housing sector, it will stay high in other sectors such as the power sector over a longer period. But for this, the Roadmap claims, the European gas market needs more integration, more liquidity, more diversity of supply sources and more storage capacity.

To conclude, the Roadmap scenarios are rather conservative with respect to the role of gas. The economic advantages of gas today provide reasonable certainty of returns to investors, as well as low risks and therefore incentives to invest in gas-fired power stations. Moreover, if CCS is available and applied at large scale, gas may become a low-carbon technology, but without CCS, the long term role of gas may indeed be limited to a flexible back-up and balancing capacity where renewable energy supplies are variable.

2.5 "Fuel of choice" or "fuel of consequence"?

As can be seen from the above discussion, there is a great uncertainty as to the role of gas in the future mid- to long term European energy mix. The future is by definition uncertain, and gas could well continue to play an important – and possibly increasing – role for some decades to come. In fact, while gas was the fuel of choice over the last two decades, it could become the fuel of consequence during the next two decades. With other alternatives (i.e. the nuclear renaissance, a very strong penetration of intermittent renewables, coal with CCS) all facing problems of their own, it could well be that gas turns out to be the winner for some time to come. Natural gas presents several advantages, if compared to other options: large availability, modest cost and easy public acceptability. Moreover, gas-fired power stations have lower upfront investment costs, are quickly built and relatively flexible in their use.

In this situation of general uncertainty, the present lack of future clarity on European import requirements could postpone upstream and mid-stream investment decisions, thus potentially generating serious problems to the EU gas security of supply. Underinvestment may, indeed, threaten the adequate provision of new supplies by exporters or in the development of necessary new infrastructure due to contradictory estimates in gas demand. Taking into account that security of demand and security of supply are complementary issues in ensuring an overall balance for security of gas supply, the EU should provide clearer signals regarding to future gas demand in Europe in order to facilitate investments, both internally and externally.

3. The role of external gas suppliers

3.1 The role of Norway

Norway has always been a reliable gas supplier to Europe, but some concerns are emerging about its capability to deliver its gas supply in the long-term. The oil output of Norway peaked in 2000. As tax revenues from hydrocarbon extraction represent an important share of Norway's state budget, the declining oil output over the last decade was one of the driving forces behind Norway's impressive gas development. Norway exported in 2010 some 100 bcm of gas, almost twice the amount of a decade ago. However it is a matter of fact that Norway has not made a significant gas discovery since the discovery of the

Ormen Langen field in 1997. This field, originally assessed at above 400 bcm, has moreover recently been downgraded by 25% to 300 bcm.

Historical evolution of Norwegian gas supply (1978-2008)

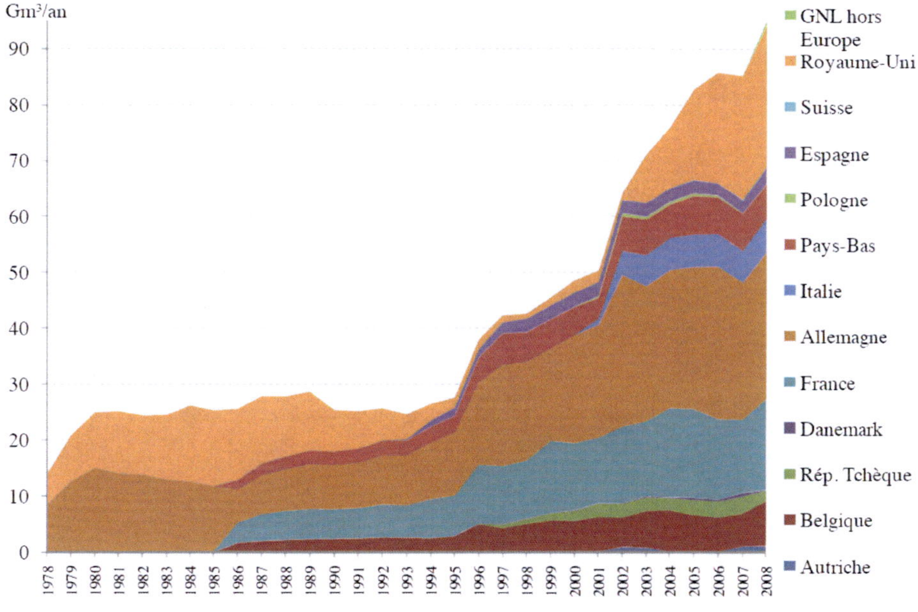

Source: IEA, Cedigaz

The Norwegian Continental Shelf (NCS), from the shoreline to internationally recommended borders measures about 2.2 million sq.kms. About one half of the NCS, ca. 1.1. million sq.kms, has rocks with a potential for finding petroleum, according to the Norwegian Petroleum Directorate (NPD). About one half of this territory (550.000 sq.kms), has in principle been opened for petroleum activities. Areas not opened yet comprise parts of the Barents Sea, parts of the Norwegian Sea close to coasts, the territory around Jan Mayen, territories offshore Lofoten and Vesterålen, as well as most of Skagerrak.

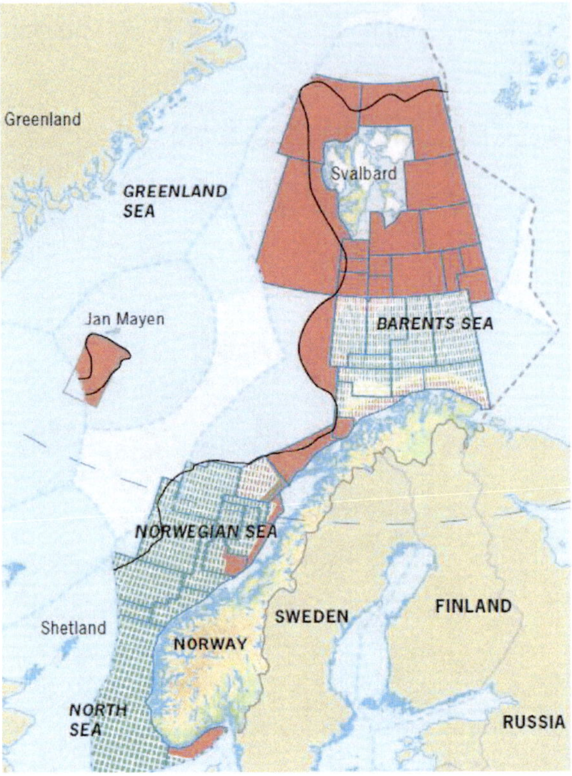

Overview of the NCS

Area status for petroleum activity on the NCS

Source: NPD

- Opened for petroleum activity
- Not opened for petroleum activity
- Activity confined to existing licences
- Exploration drilling not permitted between 1 March and 31 August
- Petroleum activity will not be initiated during this Storting (parliamentary) period
- Estimated maximum extent of sedimentary rocks which could contain petroleum

Since 1965, areas of ca. 350 000 sq.kms have been licensed, but only blocks for a total of ca. 39 000 sq.kms have been subject to exploration drilling. The major part of the area licensed is in the North Sea but not yet subject to exploration drilling making up more than 70% of the area presently at oil company disposal. Consequently, an area making up only twelve per cent of the total licensed since 1965 has been subject to exploration drilling. This apparent delay in exploration could be explained by a number of reasons: some prospective areas are not open for petroleum activities; disappointing seismic results deter companies from exploration drilling; exploration drilling has not led to discoveries judged commercially viable by the combination of reserves, assumed costs and prices; technology is seen as inadequate, so there exists a risk of delays and cost overruns. In other cases the infrastructure is not available or is too far away; and rig scarcity and the high cost of drilling under Norwegian conditions deter companies from drilling prospects that do not have top priority.

The NCS drilling story

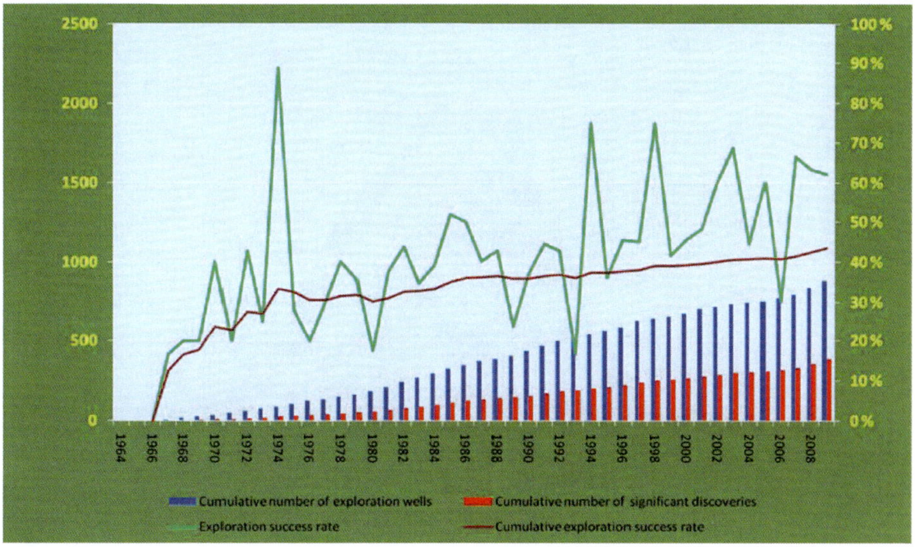

Source: NPD

There is no way to accurately predict how much gas can be produced from the Norwegian Continental Shelf. Considerable uncertainty is associated with factors such as geology, reservoir conditions, technology and knowledge development, costs and commodity prices. However, some studies have been carried out in the recent past to provide a forecast of the future Norwegian gas production. According to the Global Energy Systems Center of the University of Uppsala, Norwegian gas production will peak at a range of 124-135 bcm a year in 2015-2020 and will then fall dramatically.

Forecast of Norwegian gas production up to 2050

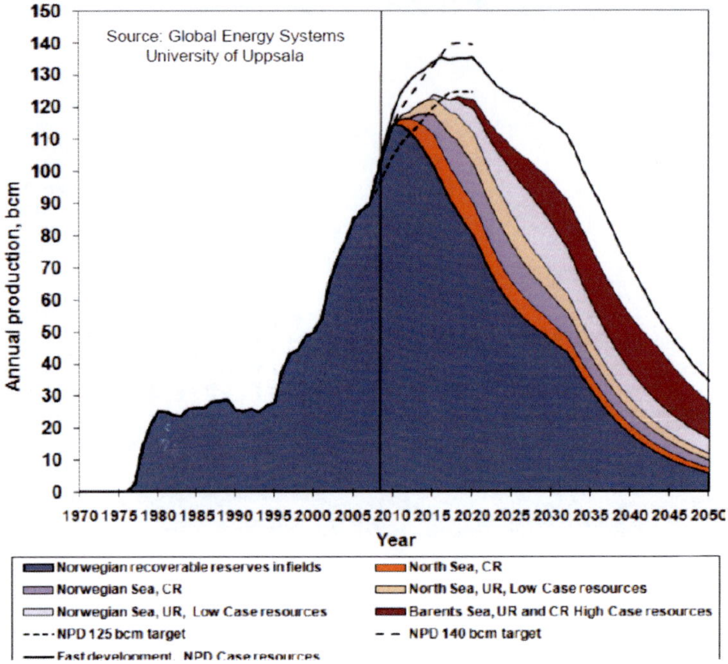

Source: University of Uppsala

According to the NPD, Norwegian gas production will peak around 2020. At that time, annual gas production is estimated at between 105 and 130 bcm a year, while the production level after 2020 will largely be determined by the new discoveries made in the years to come.

Gas production from the Norwegian Continental Shelf

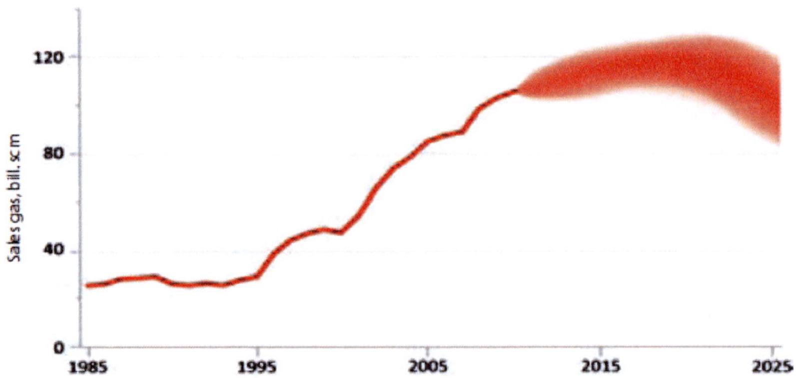

Source: Norwegian Ministry of Petroleum and Energy

The NPD has recently reviewed its own reserves and production forecasts. If large volumes of gas are found in deeply buried source rocks in the Central Graben (Ekofisk area), on the Viking Trough in the North Sea, and on the Halten Terrace in the Norwegian Sea, the NPD has reviewed its production forecast because of lower expectations following new mapping off Lofoten, Vesterålen and Senja. Here the prospects in a number of areas are smaller than previously assumed and exploration results in the Vøring Basin have failed to live up to expectations. It is also worth considering that these NPD statements may be due to strategic considerations: When reserves are limited it could make more sense to have a prudent development strategy. In other words, in an environment of temporarily low prices, why flood the market? Generally speaking, Norway will likely need to make significant discoveries in order to maintain its gas production at current levels after 2020. In this sense, it is important to mention the delimitation agreement reached in 2010 between Norway and Russia in the Barents Sea, where 175,000 sq. km. have been divided roughly 50/50 between the two countries. This promising area is now open for exploration and gathering of data.

Disputed area in the Barents Sea

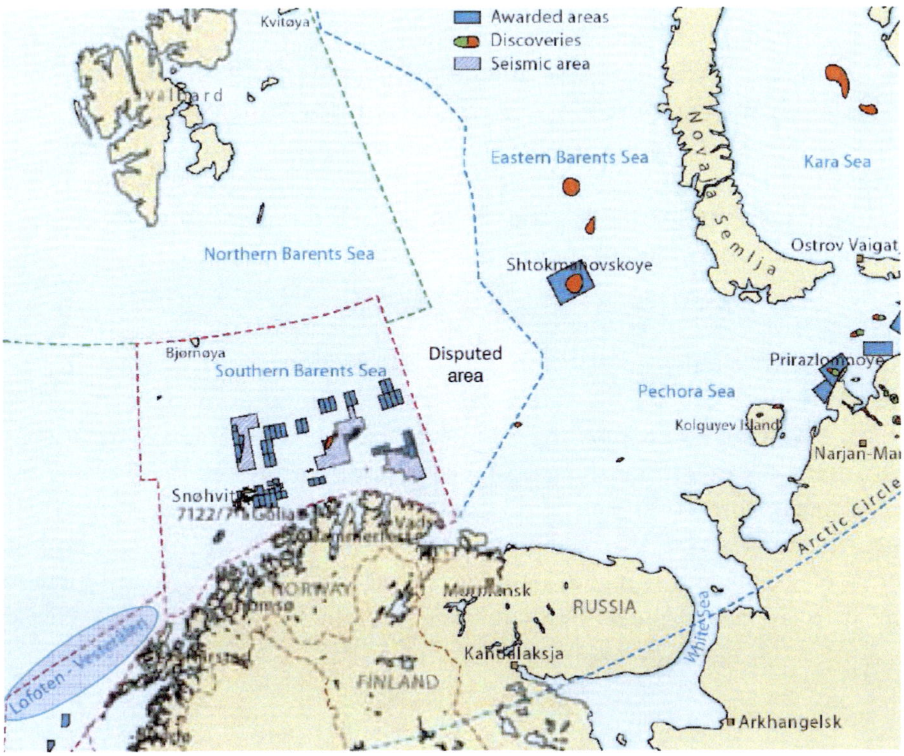

Source: NPD

Analyzing the Norwegian context it is also important to consider the more general socio-economic situation of the country. With 4,6 million inhabitants, national ownership of resources and one of the world's largest sovereign wealth funds at its disposal, the Norwegian government could also voluntarily reduce future gas production, in order to readdress the economic structure of the country away from oil and gas, and to maintain the remaining potential of natural resources available for future generations.

3.2 The role of Russia

The Russian Federation, with an amount of 45 tcm, owns 24% of the world's total proven gas reserves. Around 70% of these reserves are located in onshore Western Siberia and 10% in onshore European regions. Some 11% are located offshore on the Russian continental shelf, mainly in the Barents Sea. Around 40% of the Russian gas reserves are concentrated in hard-to-reach areas, thus making both exploration and production from the fields more technologically difficult and expensive.

Gazprom's leading position in global gas output is attributable to a handful of giant gas fields in the Nadym-Pur-Taz area in northern Tyumen Region, the shallow and compact reserves of which are easy to tap. In the 1980s and 1990s, in order to produce several hundred bcm of gas a year, it was sufficient to drill only a few thousand gas wells. These fields are largely in a declining phase obliging Gazprom to invest in new, more remote, difficult and expensive gas fields. In 1990-2004 the average annual decline in gas well flow rates was relatively stable at about 3%. The recent crisis and the following drop in gas demand explain a more substantial 3.5% decline in average gas well flow rates in 2005-09.

Russia is investing as never before in gas production. All large-scale projects are continuing despite the unfavorable market conditions since the 2009 crises. New markets are opening up in Asia and LNG became a State priority with huge tax exemptions and financial support, while the share of natural gas imports from Turkmenistan has dramatically decreased. The structure of the Russian gas balance is changing in favor of the domestic market, both in terms of supply and demand. Growing prices and growing demand increase the attractiveness of the domestic market.

Historical development and forecast of Russian gas production

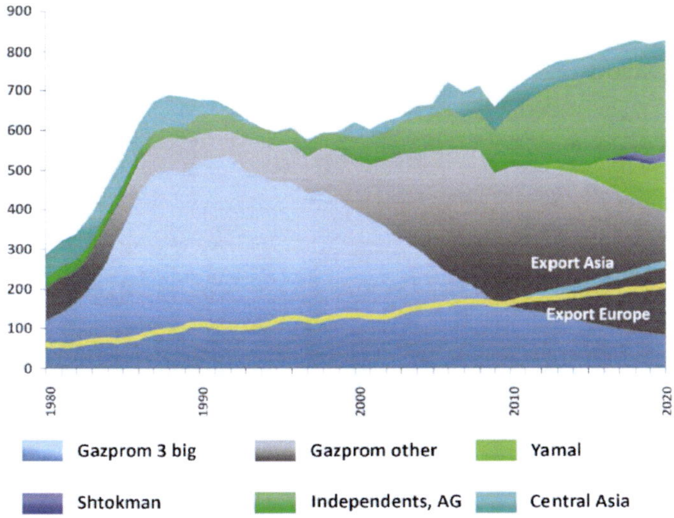

The general scheme of gas industry development of the Russian Energy Strategy up to 2030 (published by the Ministry of Energy in 2010) calls for a strong increase in production but with a wide range of production targets: 870-977 bcm by 2030 (+33-42% compared to 2008).

Indicators for the Russian gas industry development according to the ES-2030

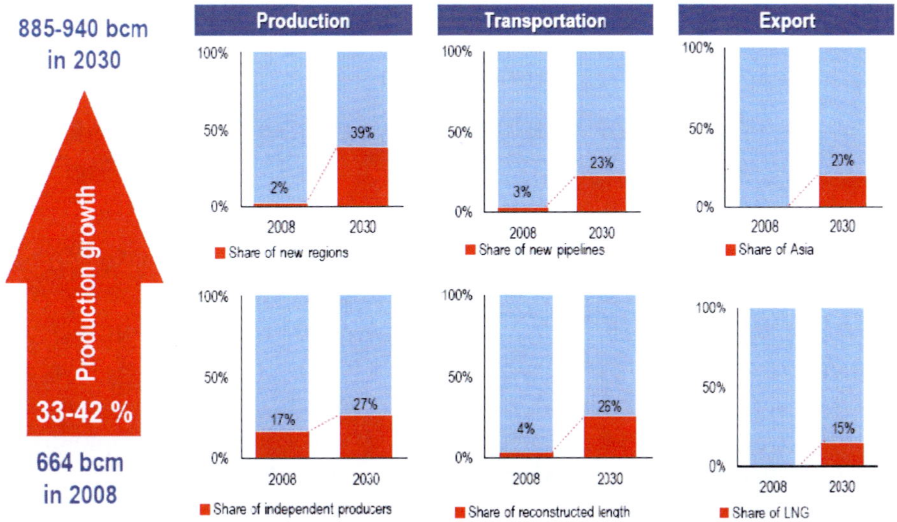

Source: Energy Strategy of Russia 2030

The share of independent companies is continuously growing. Between 1993 and 2000 it increased from 6.5% to 11.6%, and in 2010 it even reached 21.6%, thus decreasing the share of Gazprom. Among the independent producers, NOVATEK and Lukoil are the most dynamic.

Gas production in Russia (bcm)

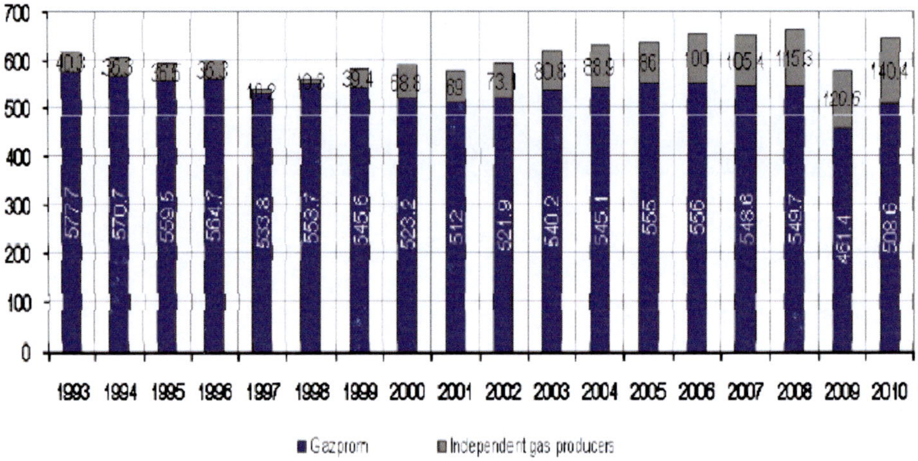

Source: Mitrova

Independent gas companies have a huge potential for production increase. According to the Energy Strategy 2030, the share of independent producers in total gas production will increase from 17% in 2008 up to 27% by 2030.

Gazprom VS. Independents production forecast (bcm)

	2011	2012	2013	2014	2015	2016	2017	2018	2019	2020
Gazprom	498.6	498.3	499.5	505.0	511.4	564.6	583.3	588.8	588.8	588.8
Independents	161.4	171.7	174.5	189.0	205.6	168.0	164.9	175.0	190.6	209.2

Independents have ambitious plans limited only by access to Gazprom's Unified Gas Suppy System (UGSS). They are expected to be able to increase production by 30-40 bcm in 1-1.5 years. In order to sustain and increase production, companies will have to move to more remote and challenging fields with significantly higher costs. The share of the new regions in the total gas production is expected to increase up to 40% due to the development of fields in Yamal, East Siberia and the Far East and the Shtokman field. At the same time, gas output will half in the developed regions.

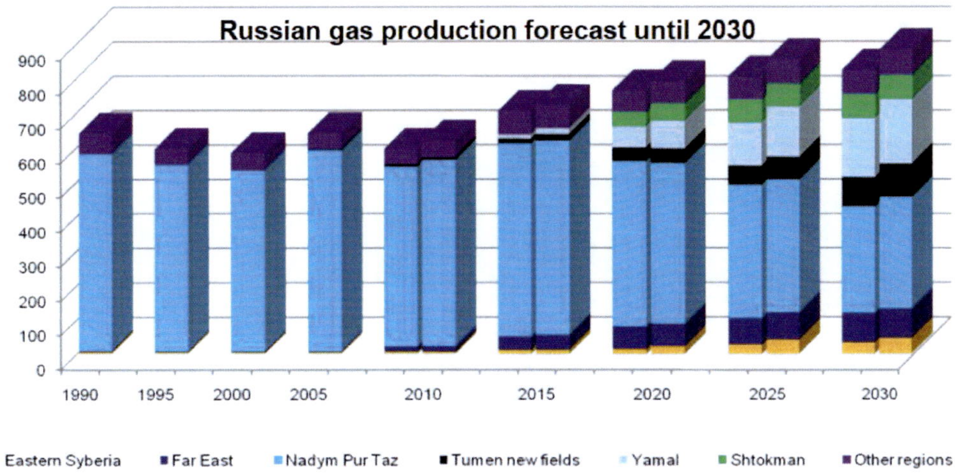

Source: Energy Strategy of Russia 2030

Russian domestic gas prices are rising to reach an equal profitability level with export prices (originally planned for 2011), but the speed of their growth will be subject for numerous reviews (due to the unpredictability of oil prices and European gas prices, changing domestic economic situation, etc.). Due to the crises and social pressure, the prices will probably reach European netback parity only in 2014. As a result, gas and coal prices will stay nearly equal until 2010-2012, returning to their normal correlation after 2015. The following graph shows the Russian domestic gas demand projection. In 2009, due to the crisis, demand declined by 6%. It is expected that gas demand will recover to pre-crises levels after 2013.

Russian domestic gas demand forecast, Innovative scenario (bcm)

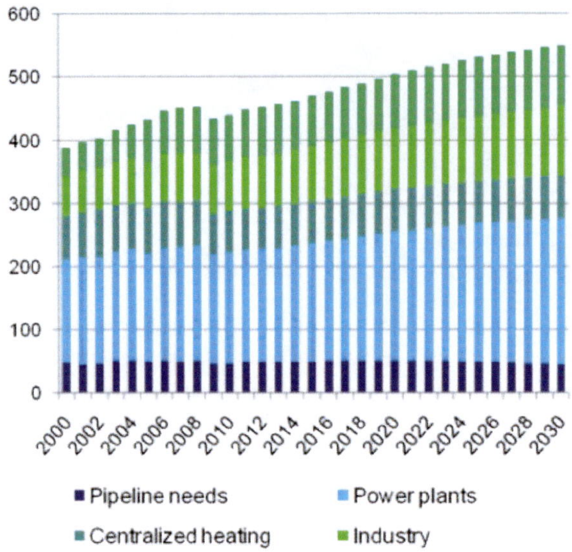

Source: Energy Strategy of Russia 2030

Projected domestic demand is expected to grow strongly as price elasticity of the domestic gas demand is rather low and as alternatives to replace gas are limited. For gas producers, the domestic price increase is the most important source of additional revenues. In 2009 for the first time Gazprom's profit from domestic gas sales reached US$ 70 billion. Increasing domestic gas prices are making domestic market more attractive and profitable for Gazprom and independent gas producers.

Concerning Russian external energy relations, the key points of the new Russian Energy Strategy are: (i) Reflecting the Russian national interests in the international energy regulation system ("New Concept of international energy markets regulation"); (ii) Export markets diversification (share of the Asian region in the Russian energy export should increase up to 26-27% in parallel with sustained volumes of energy resources to Europe); (iii) Diversification of the energy export structure, increasing share of high value-added goods (LNG share in gas exports should reach 14-15% by 2030, the share of primary energy resources in total energy exports should not exceed 70%); (iv) Provide stable conditions on the export markets, including guaranteed demand and reasonable prices for Russian energy resources (long-term take-or-pay contracts, transit agreements, by-passing infrastructure, strategic oil reserve, oil exchanges with pricing in Roubles, Russian oil markers); (v) Strengthening positions of the Russian energy companies abroad (presence of one Russian energy company among 3 world leading energy companies and among 5 leading companies; presence of two Russian companies among 10 leading energy companies and 10 leading companies); (vi) Provide efficient international cooperation on risky and challenging projects in Russia (including offshore projects in Arctic); (vii) The share of foreign direct investments in total investments in the Russian energy sector should be at least 12%, Russian companies should at the same time actively participate in the foreign projects.

Europe is a highly solvable and well-placed market for Russian gas. Minimum annual quantities of gas in Gazprom's portfolio of signed long-term contracts ensure deliveries of more than 3 tcm of gas to Europe during the period 2010-2035. Europe is already a mature market approaching plateau demand in the foreseeable future and the Russian goal is to maintain the existing market share. A downstream strategy in order to secure demand and to get additional margins could have the following structure: (i) Development of marketing and trading activities (GMT: Gazprom Marketing & Trading). Swap operations with WINGAS, DONG, Statoil and other companies in order to reach attractive North European markets, especially the UK; (ii) Swaps of assets with European companies (like WINGAS, EON, Gasunie etc.) in order to strengthen downstream positions; (iii) Power generation and direct access to the final consumers to guarantee security of demand and get additional margins; (iv) Underground storages to cover seasonal demand and increase margins.

The first priority of the Russian Energy Strategy 2030 is to maintain market share in Europe while diversifying energy supplies and decreasing dependence on European customers. The target is to increase the share of energy export to Asian markets by 20% of gas exports by 2030. Practically it means that once an agreement on gas price is reached, development of a pipeline to China will be fast.

Future Russian export capacity: diversifying export markets

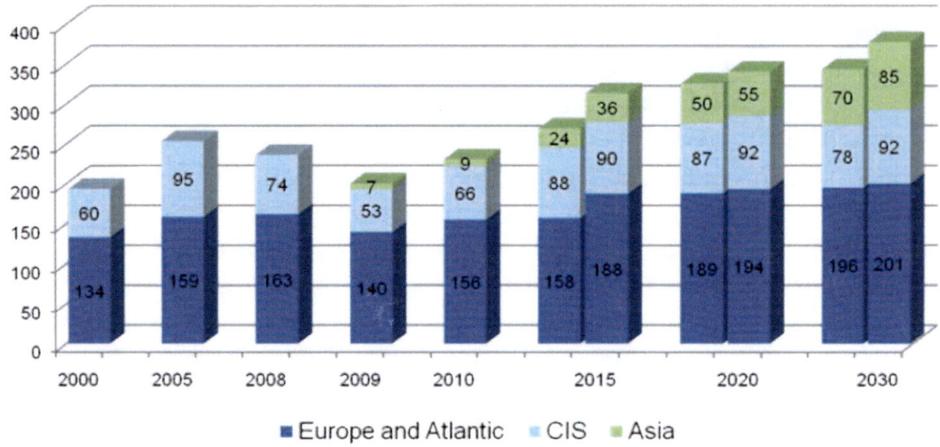

Source: Energy Strategy of Russia 2030

If Europe will remain the main export market for Russian gas, its share in the structure of Russian gas export will decrease due to an increase in supplies to Asia. European export volumes will finally depend on its market situation, not on the Russian production limits. In this sense a more stable security of EU gas demand will have, once more, a positive outlook for the EU gas security of supply. A final noteworthy initiative is the "Roadmap of the EU-Russia Energy Cooperation until 2050". On February 24 2011, the two coordinators of the EU-Russia Energy Dialogue, the European Commissioner for Energy, Günther Oettinger, and the Minister of Energy of the Russian Federation, Sergej Shmatko, signed a Common Understanding on the preparation of a roadmap that should concentrate on an analysis of different scenarios and their impact on EU-Russia energy relations, in order to investigate the potential for long-term cooperation in the field of energy. According to the "Progress report" of December 2011, the way forward for the EU-Russia Energy Dialogue would be based on three key-points: (i) To maintain and improve infrastructure connections, through a strong legal framework for cross-border investments in joints projects; (ii) To create a common energy market, through the gradual approximation of rules, standard and markets in the field of energy; (iii) To make a cleaner energy sector, with an improved cooperation on energy efficiency, renewable energy and low carbon technologies.

With regard to natural gas, the report outlined the following areas of cooperation: Upstream investment; gas flaring; market structures; infrastructure; innovative use of gas; decarbonisation; and energy efficiency. Moreover, the expert groups suggested that, in order to have successfully outcomes in the field, the EU and Russia should: (i) co-operate to maximize upstream potential by allowing a more varied and technologically advanced exploitation of the upstream; (ii) Exchange best practice and foster co-operation to address the regulatory, commercial and technological barriers to ensure improvement in natural gas utilization efficiency with a common Russia and EU objective to prevent air pollution and waste of valuable natural resources, including with respect to associated gas; (iii) Exchange information on the modernization of existing pipelines in order to decrease the losses of gas; (iv) Share all current research and development findings and plans regarding CCS; (v) Discuss and coordinate R&D in relation to the supply and transportation of gas; (vi) Share information about any new policy measures and the potential impact on the business environment before implementation; (vii) Seek a bilateral agreement regarding all natural gas export pipelines from the Russian Federation to the EU, whether direct or indirect, solving conflicts of laws and providing a framework for enhanced integration of the gas markets of the EU and Russia. Also the establishment at the end of 2011 of an EU-Russia Gas Advisory Council deserves encouragement, gathering high level experts to assess developments in the EU and Russian gas markets and to make recommendations for long-term cooperation.

3.3 The role of MENA countries

There has been talk in the past few years about the potential for the MENA region to help the EU in its drive and efforts to diversify from the suppliers it thinks it is over-dependent on. This interest has been amplified by the recent Arab uprising, a sequence of events that will possibly have an impact on the region's medium to long term energy outlook.

Share of MENA gas in EU imports (2000-2010

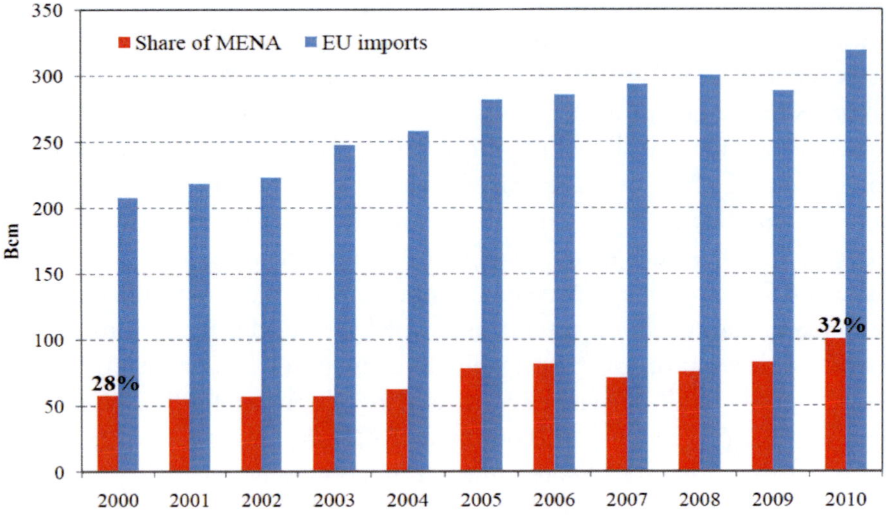

Source: Darbouche and Fattouh

In 2010 the MENA region accounted for 32% of EU natural gas imports, a level slightly higher than the 28% recorded ten years before. The region holds over 90 tcm of proven gas reserves, representing half of the world's proven gas reserves (187 tcm at the end of 2010). Moreover, with the upstream potential of most countries in the region underexplored, a lot more conventional and unconventional gas resources remain to be discovered.

3.3.1 Algeria

Algeria has 4.5 tcm of proven gas reserves and BP estimates that in 2010 its commercial gas production reached a level of 80 bcm, of which 70% was exported and 30% was consumed domestically. Algeria's largest gas field is Hassi R'Mel, discovered in 1956. Hassi R'Mel accounts for about a quarter of Algeria's total dry natural gas production, while other gas reserves come from associated and non-associated fields in the south and southeast regions of the country. Algeria's domestic pipeline system centers on the Hassi R'Mel natural gas field. The largest pipeline systems connect Hassi R'Mel to LNG export terminals along the Mediterranean Sea. Hassi R'Mel is the hub of Algeria's entire natural gas transport network, so pipelines connect to it from the country's major natural gas-producing regions. Almost two-thirds of Algeria's total natural gas exports currently move through three natural gas pipeline connections operating between Algeria and Europe; the remaining one-third of total natural gas exports is exported in the form of LNG. The export pipelines are the Enrico Mattei Pipeline (from Hassi R'Mel, via Tunisia and Sicily, to mainland Italy), the Pedro Duran Farell Pipeline (from Hassi R'mel via Morocco to mainland Spain) and the MEDGAS pipeline which became operational early 2011 (connecting directly Spain to Algeria across the Mediterranean without any transit country). Domestic demand grows strongly in Algeria, while the country found it difficult to increase production in recent years. Exports have thus been declining. In 2010 Algeria exported natural gas mainly to Italy (28 bcm), Spain (12 bcm), France (6 bcm), Turkey (4 bcm). Minor volumes went to the United Kingdom, Portugal and Tunisia.

3.3.2 Libya

Libya's proven natural gas reserves are estimated at 1.5 tcm and, as will be explained below, recent new discoveries are expected to raise these estimates in the near-term. Libya's natural gas production has grown substantially in the last few years, reaching a level of 15.8 bcm in 2010. Natural gas currently accounts for 45% of the country's generated electricity. In the past the Libyan government planned to increase the natural gas production in order to expand the use of this fuel in the power sector for freeing up more oil for export. However, project delays (also due to the recent political turmoil) and infrastructure limitations have kept consumption in this sector relatively stable over the past years. In 2010 Libya exported 9.41 bcm of natural gas to Italy (via pipeline) and 0.34 bcm to Spain (via LNG). Natural gas is piped from the Wafa concession and the offshore Bahr es Salam fields to Melitah, where it is treated for export. The amount of natural gas exports to Italy has grown considerably over the past several years through the 540 kms long "Greenstream" underwater natural gas pipeline from Melitah to Gela in Sicily, operated by Eni in partnership with Libya's National Oil Corporation (NOC).

3.3.3 Egypt

Egypt's natural gas sector has expanded rapidly with production quadrupling between 1998 and 2009. Egypt's estimated proven gas reserves stand at 2.2 tcm, representing the third largest reserves in Africa after Nigeria (5.3 tcm) and Algeria (4.5 tcm). In 2010 Egypt produced roughly 61.3 bcm of natural gas, of which 45.1 bcm consumed domestically. In 2010, Egypt exported 15.1 bcm of natural gas (of which 9.71 bcm via LNG and 5.46 bcm via pipeline).

Egyptian pipeline exports mainly travel through the Arab Gas Pipeline, an infrastructure of 1.200 km that provides gas to Lebanon, Jordan and Syria. In addition, a subsea gas pipeline -the Arish-Ashkelon Pipeline- connects the country with Israel. Egypt's LNG exports are based on the large Damietta and Idku liquefaction plants. This combined LNG export capacity is close to 23.4 bcm per year. In 2010 Egypt exported natural gas via LNG mainly to Spain (2.62 bcm), United States (2.07 bcm), South Korea (0.97 bcm), France (0.73 bcm) and Italy (0.72 bcm), while minor volumes went to Japan, Kuwait, Turkey, Belgium, UK, Greece and China. In the same year, Egypt exported natural gas via pipeline to: Jordan (2.52 bcm), Israel (2.10 bcm), Syria (0.59 bcm) and Lebanon (0.15 bcm).

3.3.4 Qatar

With proven gas reserves of about 25 tcm, Qatar has the third largest gas reserves in the world (almost the same size than those of Iran) and a population of 1.7 million (while Iran's population is about 75 million). Qatar has experienced a rapid economic growth over the last decades, with an economic policy focused on developing its huge natural gas reserves, becoming over the last decade not only -by far- the world's largest supplier of LNG but also the country with the world highest per capita income. The majority of Qatar's natural gas is located in the massive offshore North Field. In 2010 Qatar produced 117 bcm of gas, four times the amount produced in 2000. In the same year Qatar exported 95 bcm of gas, of which 76 bcm via LNG. Primary destinations for Qatar's gas exports in 2010 were: the UAE (17 bcm), the United Kingdom (14 bcm), Japan (10 bcm), South Korea (10 bcm), India (10 bcm), Belgium (6 bcm), Spain (6 bcm) and Italy (6 bcm). Qatar is a dynamic country with a wide international horizon. The latest example of this feature is represented by the engagement of the country in a discussion with Russia's biggest independent gas producer Novatek for buying a stake of the company and its 15mn tons/ year Yamal LNG – a major project expected to be devoted to the European market- an operation that would link the world's largest gas producer with the world's largest LNG exporter, creating an innovative prospect of cooperation.

3.3.5 Iran

Considering its potential in term of gas export, Iran is also an important player. Iran is the second largest gas reserve holder in the world. The country holds 30 tcm of proven gas reserves, with a commercial production standing at 140 bcm in 2010. Since the Islamic revolution in 1979, the production of gas in Iran has mainly been to meet the domestic demand. At the end of 2001 Iran began to export gas to Turkey, and in 2010 it exported 7.77 bcm of gas to the country. With its expanding economy, Iranian energy demand increased at 6.8% annual average during the last decade. Large amounts of gas are injected in oil fields to increase oil reservoir pressure to maximize oil exports. Natural gas has become the most important source in the Iranian energy mix, making the country the third-largest gas consumer in the world. Domestic natural gas demand has increased at an average rate of 10%/year over the last decade. The country has also several LNG export projects on its drawing board, but unless there is a change to a more cooperative international approach, the realization of any of these Iranian export projects will be a huge challenge.

3.3.6 Iraq

Iraq's proven natural gas reserves were estimated at 3.2 tcm in 2010. The country's natural gas production has decrease substantially over the last decade, from 3.2 bcm in 2000 to 1.3 bcm in 2010. Some of the extracted natural gas is used as fuel for power generation, and some is re-injected to enhance oil recovery. Over 40% of the production in 2008 was flared due to a lack of sufficient infrastructure to utilize it for consumption and export. For this reason, in November 2011 Iraq signed a final deal with Royal Dutch Shell and Mitsubishi to capture flared gas at southern oilfields (Rumaila, as well as Zubair and West Qurna), a project that should boost production of needed electricity.

The Iraqi natural gas outlook seems to be radically changing because of the enormous gas finds recorded in Kurdistan. In fact, between 2,8 and 5,6 tcm of gas resources are estimated to be located in the semi-autonomous territory at the confluence of Iraq, Iran and Turkey. Once established, Kurdistan's gas reserves would first be exploited to fuel new power plants in the region. In fact, the Kurdistan Regional Government has already more than tripled its 2015 target for installed gas-fired generating capacity. However, the region's gas potential seems to be so large that the only way to monetize it fully will be to develop export capacity. Consequently, Turkey would be the natural direction for exports of gas from the region to the European market.

As an overall trend, Iraq's plans to export natural gas remain controversial due to the amount of idle and sub-optimally-fired electricity generation capacity in the country. Prior to the 1990-1991 Gulf War, Iraq exported natural gas to Kuwait. The gas came from Rumaila through a 170 km, 4 bcm/y pipeline to Kuwait's central processing center at Ahmadi. In 2007, the Ministry of Oil announced an agreement to fund a feasibility study on the revival of the mothballed pipeline. Iraq has eyed northern export routes such as the proposed Nabucco pipeline through Turkey to Europe, and in 2009 Prime Minister Nouri al-Malikie suggested that Iraq could be exporting 15 bcm/y to Europe by 2015. A second option is the Arab Gas Pipeline (AGP) project. The proposed AGP pipeline would deliver gas from Iraq's Akkas field to Syria and then on to Lebanon and the Turkish border, and then on to Europe. Other proposals have included building LNG exporting facilities in the Basra region.

3.3.7 A region largely under-explored

The MENA region is endowed with a large amount of gas, but its global share in terms of supply and export remains below its potential. In fact, the overall gas production of the MENA region represented in 2010 only the 20% (669 bcm) of the world total gas production. Moreover some MENA countries are facing gas shortages, despite their considerable proven gas reserves. As mentioned above, gas consumption is growing rapidly in the region -mainly driven by electricity demand- and to date 72% of the gas produced in the region is consumed locally; which explains why the MENA region plays, today, a relatively modest role in international gas trade.

MENA vs. World gas pipeline exports (1999-2010

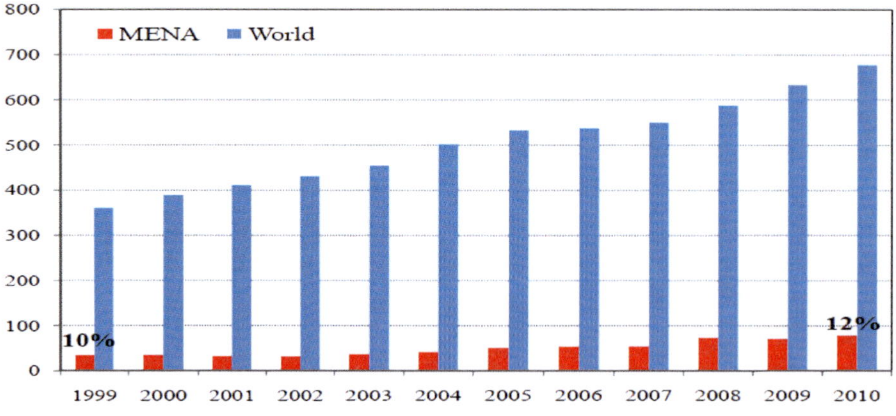

Source: Darbouche and Fattouh

MENA vs. World gas LNG exports (1999-2010)

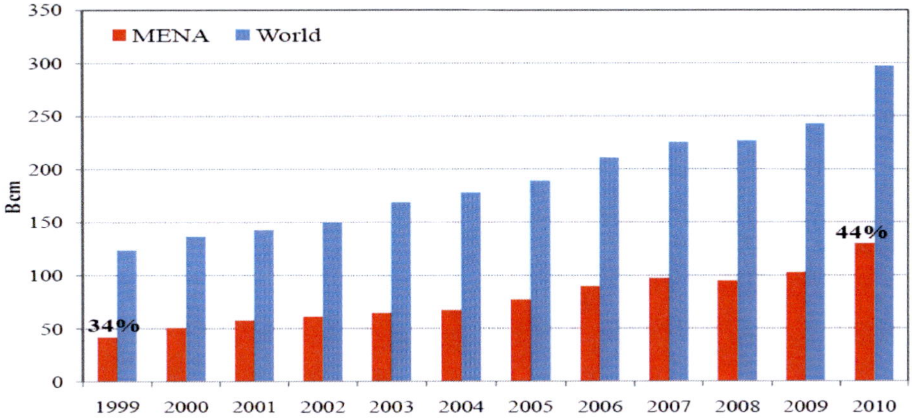

Source: Darbouche and Fattouh

As mentioned above, the region is still largely under-explored. A first example is represented by Egypt. In 2010 the US Geological Survey estimated that in the offshore in the Mediterranean-Nile offshore there is a potential for resources to be discovered which amounts at 6321 bcm of natural gas, 1.763 Gb of oil, and 5.9 Gb of NGL. If these figures will be confirmed, the area would become a world-class natural gas province.

Undiscovered resources in the Mediterranean-Egyptian Nile delta offshore

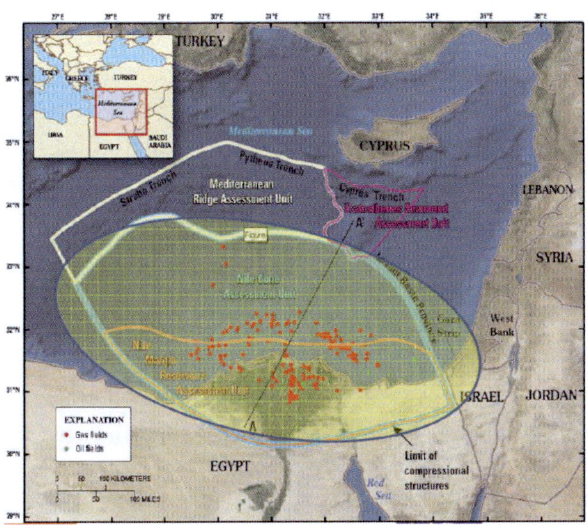

Source: US Geological Survey

A second example is represented by the Levantine Basin. A recent exploratory activity in the offshore area encompassed between Israel and Cyprus has confirmed major natural gas fields that could radically change the energy outlook of the area. Israel's Natural Gas Authority estimates that these offshore gas reserves could reach 1.3 tcm within the next few years.

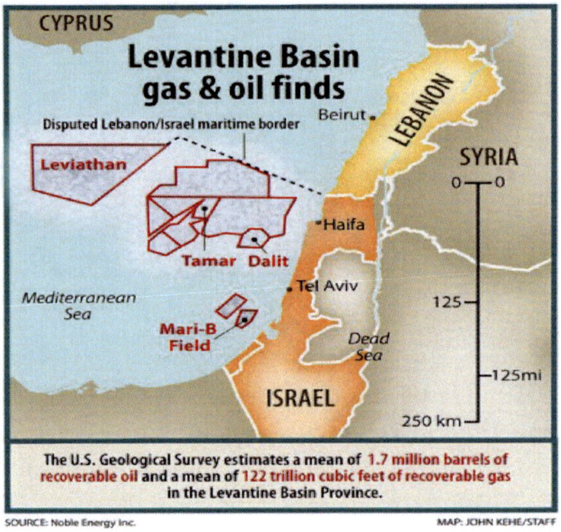

Source: Noble Energy Inc.

A large natural gas field – the so-called "Leviathan field" – with estimated reserves at 453 bcm has been discovered in late 2010 and is expected to be operative in 2017. The Cyprus Energy Department has already submitted to the Cypriot government a proposal to cooperate with Israel for the construction of an LNG plant near Vassilikos, on the island's southern coast. Noble Energy and Israel's Delek Group have proposed the construction of a 15mn tons/year LNG facility that would process gas from the Leviathan field and any gas from offshore Cyprus.

A third example off untapped resources is represented by Libya and Tunisia. Using a geology-based assessment methodology, the U.S. Geological Survey estimated 3.97 billion barrels of undiscovered oil, 1.100 bcm of undiscovered natural gas, and 1.47 billion barrels of undiscovered NGL in the Sirte Basin in Libya, in the Pelagian Basin in Tunisia and in western Libya. About 85 % of the mean total of undiscovered gas and 89 % of the mean total of undiscovered NGL are estimated to be in the Sirte Basin Province.

Locations of the Sirte and Pelagian Basin Provinces, North Africa

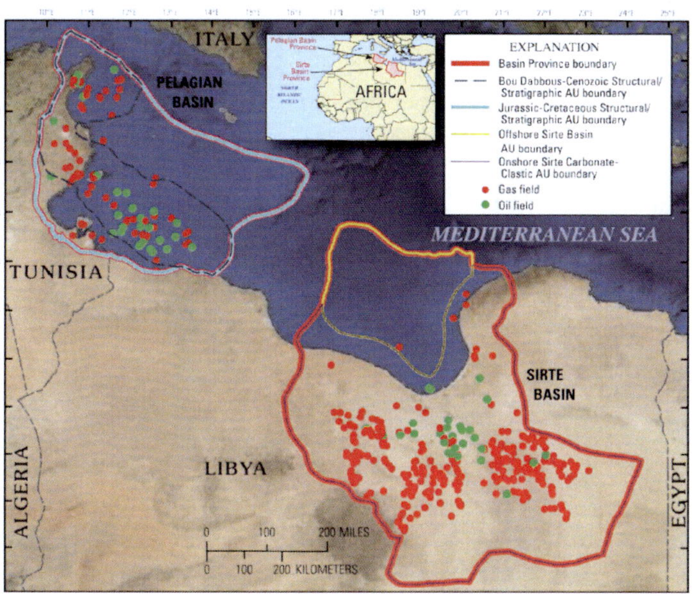

Source: US Geological Survey

The recent Arab uprisings may have an important impact also on the MENA gas markets. Three main issues seem to be fundamental for the development of gas in these countries: (i) subsidies, (ii) export policies, (iii) investment terms. However, considering the current high domestic social tensions, it seems to be very difficult for most governments in the region to deal with domestic pricing reforms. For this reason any reform in this sense will likely be delayed, leading to an increase in domestic gas consumption and thus to a constraint of gas exports in the near future.

3.3.8 A great solar energy potential

If the EU is committed to improve cooperation with the MENA region, it is important not to be perceived only as a hydrocarbon buyer but as a full-fledged partner. In this sense, the recent Arab uprisings could provide the EU with the opportunity to play a more meaningful role in the region in the future. Considering that there is not a lack of infrastructure to import gas from the MENA region to Europe, efforts towards energy efficiency and renewable energy could represent the key elements of an EU foreign energy policy towards the region. An approach based on these two priorities would provide the double dividend of accompanying sustainable economic development in the MENA countries and, at the same time, to free gas for export. Concerning the development of renewable energy in the Southern and Eastern Mediterranean countries, two important projects have been promoted over the last two years: The Mediterranean Solar Plan (MSP) and Desertec. Such large-scale renewable energy projects are strictly related to the development of gas markets. In fact, North Africa's solar potential should be devoted to satisfy the rapidly increasing domestic electricity needs in the area and thus liberating additional gas exports to Europe.

The MSP was launched in July 2008 within the framework of the Union for the Mediterranean as one of the strategic processes aimed at pursuing sustainable development of the Euro-Mediterranean region. The primary objective of the MSP is to provide 20 GW of installed capacity from renewable sources (mainly solar and wind) by 2020 and to develop electricity networks and interconnections between the two shores of the Mediterranean and between the MED-11 countries itself. Furthermore, the MSP include energy efficiency and technology transfer as accompanying measure. The objectives of the MSP are in line with the goals of the EuroMed Partnership initiated in 1995 with the Barcelona Declaration, which aims at promoting regional trade integration, infrastructure networks and improved environmental protection. In addition, the EuroMed Energy Priority Action Plan established at the Limassol Conference for the period 2008-2013 features the promotion of renewable and sustainable energy, as well as improvements to the institutional, legislative and political framework that governs the development and dissemination of renewable energy technologies. The priority areas of action of the MSP are: (i) Setting up of an adequate legal, regulatory, institutional and organizational framework to enable the development and massive deployment of solar energy and other renewable energy technologies; (ii) Limiting the growth of energy demand and improve energy efficiency and energy savings; (iii) Promote the development of electricity interconnections to establish a viable grid system for "Euro-Mediterranean green electricity" trade; (iv) Facilitate co-operation on technology aspects. The MSP has the support of the European Commission, which is accompanying this initiative through capacity building projects such as "Paving the Way for the Mediterranean Solar Plan", aimed at contributing to the establishment of harmonized legislative and regulatory frameworks for renewable energy, improving knowledge transfer and enhancing capacity building.

Desertec is an industrial initiative promoted by twelve companies, which involves the construction of concentrating solar power systems over 17000 sq. kms. of the Sahara desert in order to generate 50 GW of installed CSP capacity by 2050, that would be distributed to Europe and North Africa through a high voltage super grid. The basic idea of the initiative is that these technologies can meet the growing demand for power production and seawater desalination in the MENA region, and produce clean electrical power that can be transmitted via High Voltage Direct Current (HVDC) transmission lines with relatively little transmission loss to Europe. The Desertec initiative has the support of the European Commission, through the project "Paving the Way for the Mediterranean Solar Plan" but also through its financial support to the European Investment Bank's Facility for Euro-Mediterranean Investment and Partnership (FEMIP) and the Neighbourhood Investment Facility (NIF).

Desertec

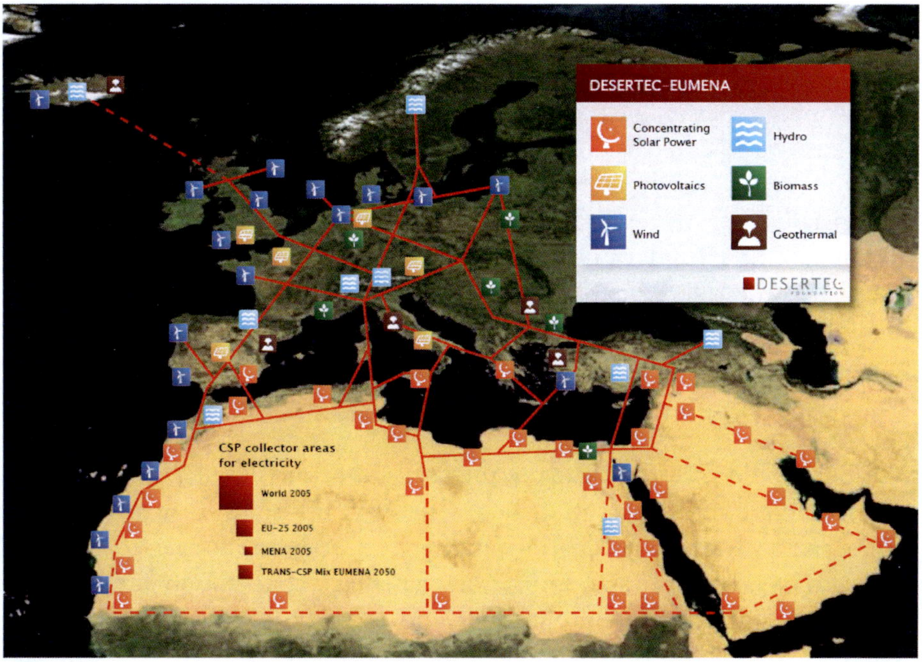

Source: Desertec foundation

All Southern and Eastern Mediterranean countries have embarked during the last years – with the support of the European Union – on an energy pathway focusing on an increased development of renewable energies and of energy efficiency. Also Algeria, the most important gas exporter of North Africa, has at the end of 2010 announced an ambitious solar programme declaring that by 2030 the country wants to produce about one quarter of its electricity out of solar thus potentially liberating gas for export. In fact, Algeria's state owned energy supplier Sonelgaz has signed in February 2012 an agreement with the Desertec Industrial Initiative to generate 22 GW of renewable energy by 2020.

Indeed, from a macro-economic point of view, it makes sense that before exporting solar electricity from North Africa to Europe, North Africa's solar potential should first be devoted to satisfy the rapidly increasing domestic electricity needs in North Africa and thus liberating additional gas exports to Europe. Transporting gas is cheaper than transporting electricity and from a public acceptability point of view it is easier to transport gas in pipelines than electricity through overhead power lines. By the way, also from a EU energy security of supply point of view, gas imports are perceived as less problematic than electricity imports. The solar development in North Africa could be financed by swaps with increased gas supply to Europe The main difficulty of swapping renewable electricity for the domestic gas consumption, which could thus be exported, is that presently domestic energy prices are much lower than the export price to European markets. As at the same time it is politically and socially difficult to align domestic energy prices to international prices, a compensation fund would have to be created to remunerate renewable electricity producers which sell the electricity on subsidized domestic markets thanks to sales of gas which is no longer sold on low priced domestic market but on the high priced international markets. In a second phase, direct solar electricity export to Europe could indeed be envisaged.

The EU should try to accompany the creation of the broader economic and political frameworks that, after the recent Arab uprisings, new governments in the region will aim to develop. Indirectly through that role, the EU will thus also be able to have an impact on the energy cooperation and therefore contributing to ensure European energy security. Cooperation with the MENA region is fundamental for the EU and energy will be one of the key vectors on which trust between the parties should be built upon.

4. The role of the Caspian Basin

The Caspian basin is endowed with a considerable amount of proven gas reserves. In 2010 Turkmenistan held 8 tcm of proven gas reserves, followed by Kazakhstan (1.8 tcm), Uzbekistan (1.6 tcm) and Azerbaijan (1.3 tcm). However, the export potential of Caspian countries is hindered by their geographical situation. Indeed, created under the Soviet era, the gas system of Turkmenistan, Kazakhstan and Uzbekistan had been designed to supply Russia. As a result, these countries remain dependent on Russia for their exports to Western regions including Europe. To directly export gas to Europe, Caspian countries would need either to have access to the Russian gas system under fair TPA conditions, or to develop alternative routes. The most important priority for the countries of the region is thus to reduce their dependence on Russia and to overcome their "landlocked" position. Therefore all of them are engaged in a number of competing pipeline projects, hoping that at least some of them would become a reality.

Main gas field and pipelines in the Caspian Basin

Source: Platts

The economic dislocation caused by the financial crisis has helped to accelerate China's economic involvement and influence in the region. The inauguration of the Turkmenistan-China gas pipeline in the end of 2009 has opened a new chapter in the regional gas trade, as Russia sells its own gas to Ukraine and Turkmenistan gas is increasingly diverted to the East. The EU is seeking to diversify both its natural gas supply and for this reason is looking at the region with interest. According to the International Energy Agency, Caspian gas production potential is expected to grow from a level of 150 bcm in 2009 to a level of 314 bcm in 2035.

Caspian gas production potential

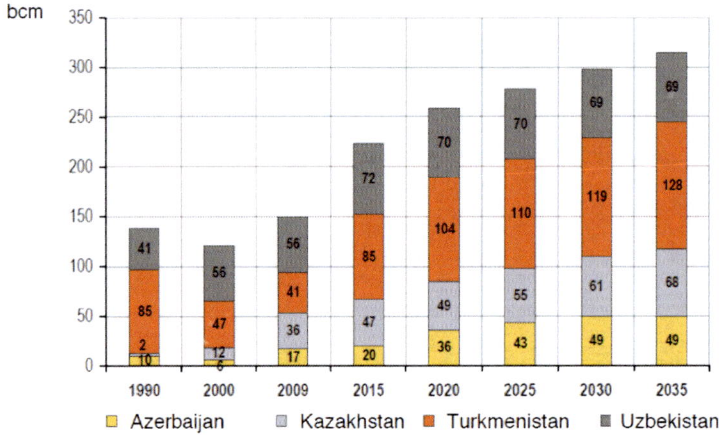

Source: IEA

According to data provided by Platts, a huge amount of gas available in the region could be potentially aggregated to feed a Southern Gas Corridor towards the EU.

Potential Suppliers for the EU's Southern Gas Corridor 2011-2020

• **Mid-2011:**	**Northern Iraq: Khor Mor & Chamchamal**	**5 bcm.**
• **2011-2013:**	**Turkmenistan: Petronas Offshore**	**5, then 10 bcm**
• **c. 2014:**	**Northern Iraq (increase on above)**	**5 bcm**
• **2015-20:**	**Turkmenistan: South Yoloten/Osman**	**10-20 bcm.**
• **c. 2016-7:**	**Iraq, Akkas**	**3-4 bcm.**
• **2016-2018:**	**Azerbaijan: Shakh Deniz-2**	**16 bcm**
• **2016-2020:**	**Azerbaijan**	**5-10 bcm**
• **2016-2020:**	**Eastern Mediterranean**	**10-20 bcm**
• **2017-2020:**	**Iraq (Baghdad-controlled) a further**	**15-35 bcm**
Total by 2020.		**80-125 bcm**

Source: Platts

Southern corridor gas pipeline projects

Source: Platts

Turkmenistan has the region's highest export potential. Once the first phase of the South Yolotan field development is completed, implementation of the second phase will commence (around 2014). This will generate an additional gas production of 10 bcm per year destined to increase further, until a peak level of 70 bcm per year by 2020-2022. Though production costs are expected to be high -up to 4$/MBtu- due to high pressure and sulfur content, part of this production could be exported towards Europe. Turkmenistan, in addition to exporting gas to China, is also interested in exporting gas to Europe. The question is thus whether it is possible to build a pipeline across the Caspian Sea. There are two major views on this point among the Caspian Sea riparian countries: (i) from Kazakhstan's, Turkmenistan's and Azerbaijan's point of view, the trans-Caspian pipeline is a matter for the countries themselves who have contiguous sub-sea boundaries; (ii) from Russia's and Iran's point of view, such a pipeline cannot be build as it does not comply with the legal status of the Caspian Sea. At the end it is a matter of practical power politics. Any pipeline under the Caspian is a delicate operation and considering its many technical and legal problems, to date it has not been possible to reach a full consensus on its feasibility.

The core gas reserves of Azerbaijan are located in Shah Deniz, the largest natural gas field of the country, situated in the South Caspian Sea. The field covers approximately 860 sq. kms and has proven gas reserves estimated to 1000 bcm. The project of Shah Deniz 2 has already been approved, and will include an additional offshore gas platform, sub sea wells and expansion to the gas plant at Sangachal Terminal. This project will add 16 bcm to the current gas production, to be exported mainly to Turkey (6 bcm) and to the EU (10 bcm).

With regard to natural gas exports from the Caspian basin to Europe (referred to as the Southern Corridor), several pipeline projects have been proposed over the last decade.

Southern Corridor proposed gas pipeline projects

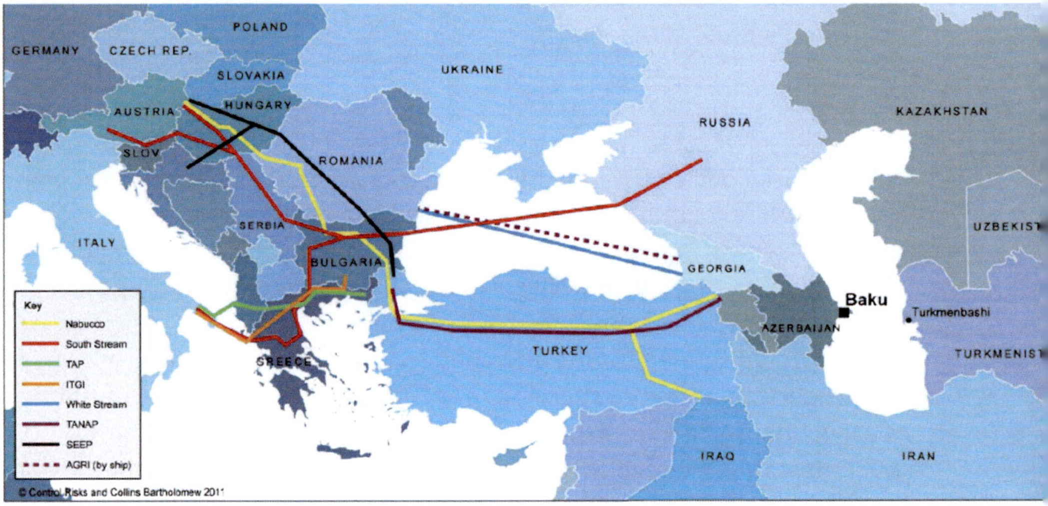

Source: Control Risks (2011)

The most ambitious and well known Southern Corridor project refers to the Nabucco project, a pipeline project running from Eastern Turkey to Austria intended to deliver gas from different countries in the Caspian Sea and the Middle East regions to Europe with a total throughput capacity of 31 bcm. The shareholders of this scheme are including Austria's OMV, Hungary's MOL Group, Bulgaria's Bulgargaz, Romania's Transgaz, Turkey's BOTAS, and Germany's RWE. However, the Nabucco pipeline has faced great difficulties: (i) Gas availability: Nabucco is a large scale project promoted by mid-stream companies and which are looking for gas. Azerbaijan can today alone not provide the amount of gas required by Nabucco and the geopolitical situation in the Caspian and Middle-East region is today too complicated to bundle gas availabilities to be committed to this project. Nabucco has often been dubbed "a gas pipeline without gas". The competitors do either have the gas (SouthStream) or are smaller scale project which can rely on a single and smaller supply base (e.g. ITGI, TAP). (ii) Financing and guarantees: The competition between Nabucco and South Stream for the same markets, with on the one hand Southstream being promoted by a consortium of a large scale gas producer (Gazprom) and major downstream gas marketers (Eni, EDF, Wingas) which have access to the gas, who can directly market the gas and most importantly who can finance the construction on a corporate finance basis, and on the other hand Nabucco which relies on mid-size companies which need to resort to project-financing. Before investing banks require guarantees related to gas supply availability, gas demand and transport contracts. All of this is difficult in the present economic environment for a mega project like Nabucco.

With too little progress on the Nabucco pipeline project over the last years, despite all the political support from the EC, in December 2011 the governments of Azerbaijan and Turkey have signed a Memorandum of Understanding to progress with the construction of a 16 bcm per year Trans Anatolian Pipeline (TANAP), which would carry gas up from the eastern border of Turkey to the western border, likely Bulgaria or Greece and which would in a first phase rely on existing under utilized pipeline sections in Turkey, thus minimizing the sections to be fully new built. The project is currently shared by the State Oil Company of Azerbaijan (SOCAR) -which holds an 80% stake in the project- and the Turkish state company BOTAS. Further companies could farm into the TANAP project during 2012, although SOCAR will retain operatorship. Initial cost estimates for the pipeline are US$ 5 billion. Work has begun on the preparation of a feasibility study of the TANAP project. According to SOCAR, TANAP work is expected to begin by the autumn of 2012. TANAP is today considered the most likely pipeline project for the first section of the Southern Gas Corridor (from Azerbaijan to the Turkish-EU border) because it is developed by Azerbaijan which owns the gas and which has the money to finance the pipeline directly as it can draw on its accumulated oil revenues earned over the last decade. Moreover, TANAP is planned to be scalable, i.e. gradually reaching full operating capacity in step with gas production increases, so as to avoid financial losses from temporary below-capacity use.

It should also not be forgotten, that the TANAP pipeline is strategic for Azerbaijan, as it will provide Azerbaijan with control over a pipeline aimed at evacuating gas from its Shah Deniz field (and it the future possibly other Azeri fields) further down the supply chain to Europe, rather than selling at its border. As a consequence, however, there is the risk that Azerbaijan, which will the operator of the pipeline, could use the pipeline so as to avoid competing gas from the region to enter the pipeline also reach European markets.

The emergence of TANAP presented the final deathblow to the original Nabucco. In fact Azerbaijan has both the gas and the money to build. The Nabucco project has therefore recently been downgraded both concerning the capacity and length. Since TANAP will bring in a first phase about 10 bcm to the Turkish-Bulgarian border, the down-scaled Nabucco project (called Nabucco-West) would carry this gas on to Austria. The asset of Nabucco West is to benefit from the existing legal framework, namely the Intergovernmental Agreement, Project Support Agreements and third party access exemptions of the original Nabucco pipeline project as Nabucco West will follow exactly the same route on European Union territory.

Due to the frustrations with the slow progress of the original Nabucco project, in September 2011, British Petroleum (a consortium member of Shah Deniz), proposed the South East Europe Pipeline (SEEP) which was initially designed to carry Azeri gas from eastern Turkey to Austria, but after the emergence of the TANAP project it has been downscaled to transport gas from the Turkish-Bulgarian border to Central Europe. Also SEEP just like TANAP would use in a first phase existing pipelines with available capacity wherever possible, thus reducing the need of new pipeline sections to be built. SEEP is a direct competitor of Nabucco West.

Another project in the framework of the Southern corridor which has been around for a decade relates to the ITGI (Interconnector Turkey-Greece-Italy) project promoted by Greek DESFA and DEPA as well as Italian Edison. The project was composed by a Greek onshore section and an offshore leg linking the Greek Ionian coast to southern Italy. On Febraury 20, 2012 the Shah Deniz Consortium announced that the ITGI had been eliminated from the group of proposals. This because DESFA, the state owned Greek TSO, lacked to explain credibly how it intends to finance the € 1 billion onshore component and because of the missing scalability of the project.

This recent development has thus reinforced the Trans-Adriatic-Pipeline (TAP), a project to construct a new pipeline (initially 10 bcm, later possibly 20) across the territory of Greece from Komotini (near the Turkish-Greek border) to the Albanian border, across Albania and the Adriatic Sea to Italy. TAP is promoted by Statoil (a member of the Shah Deniz consortium), E.on (who has a gas market in Italy) and the Swiss energy utility EGL. With such shareholders, TAP has a credible financial support behind it.

The development of one pipeline project rather than another will primarily depend on the Shah Deniz Consortium's decision, expected for mid-2013.

Both Turkmenistan and Azerbaijan have expressed several times in the recent past the availability of substantial gas volumes and a clear willingness to sell it to Europe. The European Union seems to be ready to give the political and legal support for the gas deliveries to take place. Over the last months, the EU has engaged in a regular dialogue with Azerbaijan and Turkmenistan, which figure among the key potential gas suppliers of the Southern Corridor. However, is also important to take into consideration that -because of its historical background and its relation with Russia - Turkmenistan is not used to talking to markets - but to states. In this sense Iran, China Pakistan and India are partners with which the country could feel more at ease unlike an EU that, speaking with many voices, does not always represent a clear and unambiguous counterpart. A first step in this direction was made on September 12, 2011, when all 27 EU Member States accorded to the European Commission the mandate to negotiate a legally binding treaty between the EU, Azerbaijan and Turkmenistan to build a Trans Caspian Pipeline System.

In the meantime the situation in the region has rapidly evolved. With the rise of TANAP as the most-likely project, the EU should now work to assure that such a pipeline will be open not only to natural gas supplies from Azerbaijan but also from other producing countries, in order to preserve the principle of diversification of gas supplies, at the core of the Southern Corridor concept.

5. External dimension of the EU energy policy

The aims of the EU energy policy, as set in Article 194 of the Treaty on the Functioning of the EU, are to ensure the functioning of the energy market, to ensure security of energy supply in the Union, to promote energy efficiency and energy saving and the development of new and renewable forms of energy, and to promote the interconnection of energy networks. The Treaty postulates that these aims have to be pursued in a spirit of solidarity among member states, but it seems to be controversial when it comes to the point of the energy mix, which remains under the responsibility of each member state. This generates huge diversity not just in terms of the mix, but also in terms of relations with suppliers and in terms of policy-priorities.

Up to now, the EU has made major steps on the development of its internal energy market, but too little effort has been made in order to develop an external dimension to EU energy policy. With more than half of the gas consumed in the EU coming from third countries, a share steadily increasing and projected to reach about 80% by 2030, it is clear than none of the aims of EU policy on energy can successfully be met without taking into account major evolutions on the energy scene beyond the EU borders.

The European Commission recognized the need to strengthen the external dimension of the EU energy policy with its Communication "Energy 2020 – A strategy for competitive, sustainable and secure energy" of 10 November 2010. Moreover, the European Council of 4 February 2011 concluded that "there is a need for better coordination of Union and Member States' activities with a view to ensuring consistency and coherence in the EU's external energy relations with key producer, transit, and consumer countries". The Council therefore invited Member States to inform the Commission – starting from 1 January 2012 – of all their new and existing bilateral energy agreements with third countries. This proposal transforms the conclusions of the European Council into a mechanism with detailed procedures for the exchange of information between Member States and the Commission with regard to intergovernmental agreements, i.e., legally binding agreements between Member States and third countries which are likely to have an impact on the operation or the functioning of the internal market for energy or on the security of energy supply in the EU. The Commission would distribute the information it receives to all member states, unless it is confidential. Before an agreement enters into force, the Commission would have the right to carry out a compatibility check to verify that the deal being formulated complies with EU law. This proposal is expected to lead to more transparency and an improved ability to maintain a properly functioning EU internal energy market, safeguard energy supplies, and realize major new energy projects. Another reason is that confirming in advance whether bilateral agreements are compatible with EU Law, the Commission can also provide investors with important legal certainty.

The proposal accompanies the European Commission's Communication on security of energy supply and international cooperation "The EU Energy Policy: Engaging with Partners beyond Our Borders" of 7 September 2011. The Communication recognizes that the EU external energy policy is crucial to complete the internal energy market and underpins the 2014 deadline set by the European Council to complete the internal market for electricity and gas. It urges to unfold the EU external energy dimension to secure European energy needs, promote free and transparent energy markets, and contribute to greater security and sustainability in energy production and use.

The Communication proposes concrete ways to extend energy cooperation beyond the mere physical security of imports

(i) Building up the external dimension of EU internal energy market;

(ii) Strengthening partnerships for secure, safe, sustainable and competitive energy;

(iii) Improving access to sustainable energy for developing countries;

(iv) Better promoting EU policies beyond its borders. Such partnerships and the EU engagement in global fora -such as the G20 nations- must also promote more sustainable energy policies in third countries, while improving market transparency, easing international market volatility, and working toward a global energy market less vulnerable to supply shocks and disruptions.

The Communication also suggests that sometimes the Commission should negotiate not alongside but instead of member states: "Negotiating mandates for the EU may be necessary where agreements have a large bearing on the EU energy policy objectives and where there is a clear common EU added-value".

The first operational decision in line with this Communication is the mandate accorded on September 12, 2011 by all 27 Member States to the European Commission to negotiate a legally binding treaty between the EU, Azerbaijan and Turkmenistan to build a Trans Caspian Pipeline System. This is the first time that the European Union has proposed a treaty in support of an infrastructure project. This decision is a direct follow-up of the visit of President José Manuel Barroso and Energy Commissioner Günther Oettinger to Baku and Ashgabat in January 2011 and their meetings with Presidents Aliyev and Berdimuhamedov. In fact this is not just the first operational decision as part of a coordinated and united EU external energy strategy, but it also constitutes a milestone in the realisation of the Southern Corridor. The Trans-Caspian Pipeline agreement should set the basis for the construction of a submarine pipeline connecting Turkmenistan to Azerbaijan, and in turn link this pipeline to infrastructure that will bring gas from Central Asia to the EU. Discussions with Azerbaijan and Turkmenistan will focus on *inter alia* a treaty setting out legal commitments between the European Union; Turkmenistan and Azerbaijan; the bilateral arrangements necessary for Turkmenistan and Azerbaijan to achieve the commissioning, building; operation of the trans-Caspian pipeline itself; and the legal framework that will apply to filling the pipeline with gas from Turkmenistan, including appropriate recognition of commercial arrangements.

6. Conclusions and recommendations

This chapter has provided a wide overview on the EU external relations and its relation to gas infrastructure, analyzing the role played by Norway, Russia, the MENA region and the Caspian Basin in the EU gas security of supply chessboard.

Norway has always been a reliable gas supplier to Europe, but some concerns are emerging about its capability to deliver its gas supply in the long-term. In fact, the country has not made significant gas discoveries over the last decade. Different institutions estimate that the Norwegian gas production will peak around 2020. Also if the production level after 2020 will largely be determined by new discoveries made in the years to come, for the time being the EU should thus not expect to import considerable additional volumes of natural gas from Norway in the post-2020 period.

Russia owns the largest gas reserves of the world, is the first gas supplier of the EU and it will remain so in the future. The interdependence between the two actors is indissoluble: the EU needs Russian gas supplies as Russia needs the highly solvable European gas market. For this reason the EU should strengthen EU-Russia energy relations, in particular through the "EU-Russia Energy Dialogue". This forum represents an important occasion to investigate the potential for a long-term energy cooperation strategy that could deal with: The development of the upstream potential; the coordination of R&D in relation to the supply and transportation of gas; the discussion on new policy measures; the potential impact on the business environment. Moreover, it would be primarily important to seek a bilateral agreement regarding all natural gas export pipelines from Russia to the EU, solving conflicts of laws and providing a framework for enhanced integration of the two gas markets. In this sense, the recently established "EU-Russia Gas Advisory Council" (which gathers high level experts from the EU and Russia with the aim to make recommendations for the long-term gas cooperation between the two actors) should deserve the encouragement of all the EU institutions.

The MENA region as a whole holds half of the world's proven gas reserves. Moreover, additional conventional and unconventional gas resources still remain to be discovered. Gas consumption is growing rapidly in the region – mainly driven by electricity demand – and some countries are facing gas shortages. If the EU is committed to improve the cooperation with the region, it is important not to be perceived only as a hydrocarbon buyer but as a full-fledged partner; in this sense the recent Arab uprisings could provide the EU with the opportunity to play a more meaningful role in the region. Considering that there is not a lack of infrastructure to import gas from the MENA region to the EU, efforts towards energy efficiency and solar energy in particular, could represent the key elements of an EU foreign energy policy towards the region. In fact, an approach based on these two priorities would provide the double dividend of accompanying sustainable economic development in MENA countries and, at the same time, to free up gas for export; in this sense, the EU should strengthen its support to large-scale renewable energy projects in North Africa, such as the Mediterranean Solar Plan and Desertec. The EU should also try to accompany the creation of the broader economic and political framework that, after the recent Arab uprisings, new governments in the region will likely aim to develop. In particular the EU should be interested in developing cooperation schemes with North Africa. Contributing to the economic development of this area would have several positive spillovers, such as preventing migratory flows towards Europe, creating new markets and securing the existing gas supplies from political or social upheavals. Energy will be one of the key vectors on which trust between the parties should be built upon.

The Caspian Basin is endowed with a considerable amount of proven gas reserves. The region has an important gas export potential towards Europe, currently untapped by its "landlocked" position. Created under the Soviet era, the gas system of Turkmenistan, Kazakhstan and Uzbekistan had been designed to supply Russia. As a result, these countries remain dependent on Russia for their gas exports. Gas imports from the Caspian Basin could help Europe in diversifying its portfolio of gas supplies. However, to directly export gas to Europe, Caspian countries would need either to have access to the Russian gas system under fair TPA conditions, or to develop alternative routes. In this sense, gas infrastructure is a major topic for the area. All Caspian countries are engaged in a number of competing pipeline projects, hoping that at least some of them would become a reality. The major potential gas suppliers for the "Southern corridor", Turkmenistan and Azerbaijan, have expressed several times in the recent past their availability to supply Europe with substantial gas volumes. Over the last months, the EU has been engaged in a regular dialogue with these two countries. Given the political attitude of these states, the EU must "speak with one voice" to the region. In this sense, the EU should firmly implement the path already initiated with the mandate accorded on September 12, 2011 by all 27 Member States to the European Commission to negotiate a legally binding treaty between the EU, Azerbaijan and Turkmenistan to build a Trans Caspian Pipeline System.

Although with high level of uncertainty on the demand side, natural gas could well continue to play an important -and even increasing- role for some decades to come. While natural gas was the "fuel of choice" over the last two decades, it could become the "fuel of consequence" during the next two decades. With other alternatives all facing problems of their own (i.e. the nuclear renaissance, a very strong penetration of intermittent renewable energy sources, coal with CCS), it could well be that gas turns out to be the winner for some time to come, thus realizing the "golden age of gas" recently predicted by the International Energy Agency. However, in the case of Europe the fulfillment of this prophecy will mainly depend on two points: (i) the availability of carbon capture and storage technologies at large scale because natural gas has no future in the long-term EU energy mix unless it is fitted with viable CCS technologies; (ii) the signals that the EU provides on future gas demand. Any action in this direction would be essential in order to facilitate investments -both internally and externally- thus contributing to the reinforcement of the overall EU gas security of supply architecture.

CHAPTER II

BRINGING GAS TO AND THROUGH EU MARKETS

Jacques de Jong
Senior Fellow, Clingendael International Energy Programme (CIEP)

1. Global gas supplies to EU gas markets

1.1 Setting the supply scene

In setting the scene for this issue, a global overview was given with some focus on the three large regions in the world where gas is playing a dominant role in the fuel mix.

1.1.1 The US Market

Starting with the US, it is to be underlined that in the first decade of this century a steady growth of gas consumption took place, notably in the power sector. Furthermore, that growth brought an increase of US-consumers calling on global markets outside the US. This led to a strong increase of LNG-imports, facilitated by an expansion of LNG import-terminals. As to future demand and supply scenarios, the US-DOE's Energy Information Administration in its yearly outlooks forecasted in February 2008 a steady increase of LNG-imports up to the end of 2010. Some 16 months later that forecast was dramatically changed, leading to a stabilisation of early 2005 import-levels (figure 1). The reason for this dramatic change had everything to do with the increase of domestically produced unconventional gas. One could conclude from this for the next decade or so that a US call on global gas supplies from abroad is not likely to happen; some experts are even forecasting that the US might become an exporter of LNG to global gas markets.

Figure 1. The US Gas Supply basis

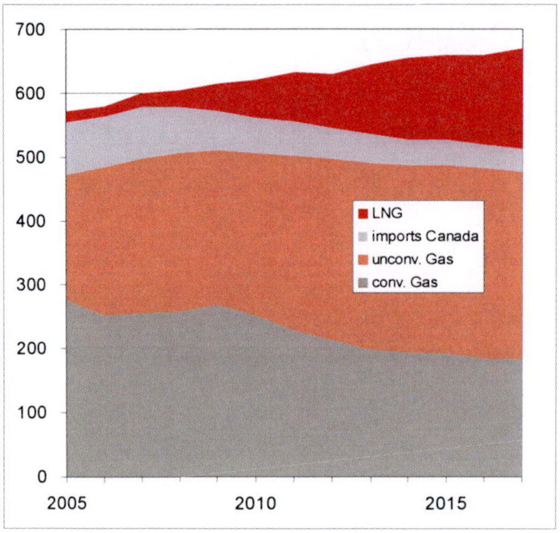

US forecasts February 2008

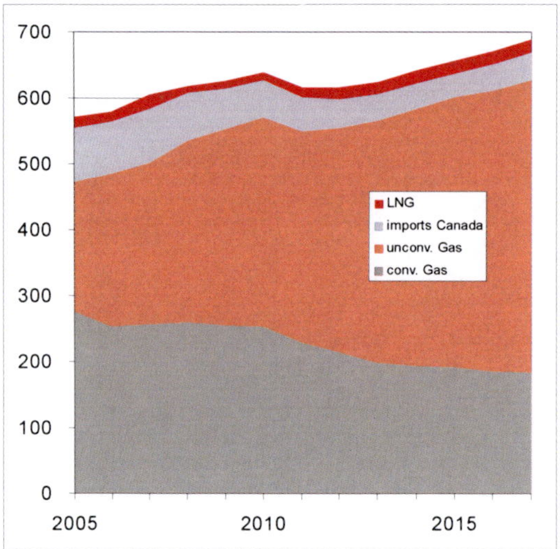

US forecasts August 2010

1.1.2 The Asian market

Existing and traditional demand for natural gas in Japan, South- Korea and emerging markets in the South-East (including India) will continue or start to play a stronger role in the region's supply-demand balances. The Fukushima incident and the resulting turmoil in Japanese energy policy making will have a further impact on the quest for gas supply in that country. Although it is too early to predict what impact the Fukushima incident will have on Japan's energy needs, it may be realistic to accept that Asian demand will continue to call on global gas markets.

More particular, especially China will increasingly focus on the role of natural gas. One might foresee that due to the need to "green" the energy supply system in China, natural gas has a major role to play. If this scenario plays out, large amounts of gas will have to be imported, especially in the high growth coastal areas. In anticipation thereof, the number of LNG importing terminals is increasing from the present 14 bcm to more than 80 bcm in 2020. China is obviously one of the fastest growing LNG-markets worldwide and suppliers from Turkmenistan to Australia are attempting to widen their share in Chinese markets.

1.1.3 The MENA region

The MENA region, covering the Middle East and North Africa, has some 45 percent of the world's remaining gas reserves, but contributes for only around 20 percent to the world's output, bringing arguments for further export potentials. However, it is faced with growing gas consumption, especially driven by the demand for power generation. Booming electricity consumption is seen as a consequence of the region's sustained economic and population growth together with artificially low prices. Hence some 70 percent of the region's gas output is consumed locally, a trend which is expected to continue into the future. Domestic markets will therefore strongly influence gas export potentials. Social pressure in the region, gathering momentum with the "Arab spring", and stalling domestic price reforms will remain key factors. Even if there are business opportunities to expand the domestic supply basis, the likelihood is that the driver will come more from a direct gas monetization policy to create domestic job opportunities in energy-intensive industries. Therefore, gas in the MENA-region will more and more become important in a domestic way, with a growing onus on resource nationalism. EU gas markets and EU consumers should therefore be realistic in their assessments of the role of gas supplies from the MENA-region.

1.1.4 Russia

Russia was, still is, and will remain the EU's primary external gas supply source, covering today some 30 percent of total EU gas consumption. Secure supplies need sufficient reserves, reliable routes to the market, the necessary upstream investments and the affordable conditions and prices to be able to respond to the actual demand. On the other side of the equation, EU markets were, are and will continue to be Russia's primary export market for its gas, covering some 70 percent of total exports with the balance made up of gas exports to the CIS and Far East. Russian gas however is still flowing for around 80 percent via a single transport route, so this would make the case as well for diversifying transport routes of that supply base as the recent opening on the 8th of November of the Nord Stream pipeline that links Russian gas export directly to its main EU import market in Germany shows. All Russian exports to the EU will remain pipeline based, and when the EU demands more gas, and this gas will come from Russia, more pipeline capacity will be needed. It is therefore relevant to focus on these transport routes, and more in particular on the potentials of the Southern Corridor and the South Stream project.

The new pipelines bringing Russian gas to EU markets, i.e. the Nord Stream and the South Stream are on the basis of joint ventures with the EU gas industry, highlighting confidence in future demand and willingness to share the risks in projects that have life-spans of several decades. This would also require mutual trust and reliability, also in political and regulatory terms. The history of the EU gas directives were not designed to be applied outside the internal EU market and the EU's external energy policy strategy was not always fit to meet its global supply security agenda. The forthcoming discussions in the EU on both the external policy dimension and the new infrastructure policy will have to take due account of the fact that new routes, such as the South Stream project or Southern Corridors, are not only bringing Russian or Caspian gas to the EU, but also through the EU (see figure 2). This would underline as well that projects should be considered as benefitting the EU gas supply basis and that those that meet the criteria that define the European interests would therefore receive the necessary priority treatment.

1.2 The South Stream

1.2.1 The project

The project, connecting Russian gas through the Black sea to South-East Europe is on track, with feasibility studies on the offshore and onshore sections being integrated and finishing early 2012. The routes coming from Russia are going through the Black Sea, the Turkish economic zone, into Bulgaria. There is still an option for landfall in Romania, but Bulgaria is the base case, with one string of line going southward via Greece with a further offshore crossing to Italy. There are still a number of options for routing through the Balkans, allowing various direct supply connections from Russia to the EU. Capacity is planned to be 63 bcm a year, translated offshore into 4 lines of 15 bcm that will gradually be taken into operation. Final investment decision is scheduled for 2012 and first supplies are planned for 2015. The gradual implementation is also important from a regulatory point of view, because the receiving infrastructures have to be put in place as well. So part of the lines will have to be built within the EU, which is for instance different compared to the Nord Stream project where the supplies are delivered on the EU-borders. This is challenging, as the FID needs not only to take into account the engineering side and the impact assessments, but also the regulatory regime needs to be clarified. This is challenging the more so as the regulatory framework is not fully clear to all market participants concerned. The Third package has not yet been implemented in any of the participating countries and it is to be understood that the projected is an integrated one, needing exact clarity on the full regulatory status.

South Stream is a privately funded project in the same way that Nordstream is. And as long as the basic idea of EU energy policy is that the networks and the supplies have to rely on private investment and not on public funds, the regulatory framework and the policy framework have to be encouraging enough to investors and their lenders to make their investment decisions on a level playing field. The budget estimation is some € 15.5 billion, of which about two-thirds has to go to the offshore section. South Stream shareholders are fully confident to be able to raise the funds necessary, with Nord Stream as a good reference case. Although being a smaller project with just an offshore section, and hence being less complicated from a regulatory point of view, Nord Stream partners were able to raise about 70 percent of the capital on the financial market, a clear indication of trust in the longer term role of import-gas in the EU energy mix.

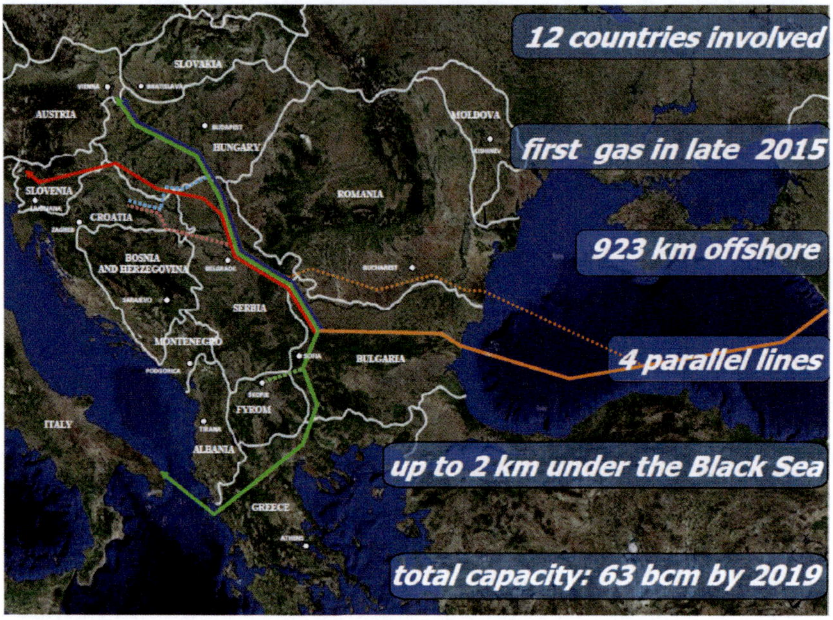

Figure 2. The South Stream project

1.2.2 South Stream and the EU internal market

South Stream has some specific characteristics with the EU internal market that would bring many observers to arguing whether or not it will go or not go. The off-shore engineering challenges are real hurdles, also with respect to the environmental impacts, but it would seem that the on-shore regulatory clarifications are the most critical ones, especially taking into account the transit-countries that are member of the EU. Here is a large difference with both Nord Stream that is "just" landing on the EU-border and Nabucco, where regulatory priority focus received large political backings at EU-levels as it regards new market entrants. The South Stream sections in the EU all have to deal with the EU's TPA-rules, where the option for exemptions might be a difficult one to get. And as long as these issues are not settled, other shippers than Gazprom, if any, might be very reluctant to book. The question may also be relevant to what extent the South Stream would be facilitating to "send back" commercially gas flows from say Baumgarten in Austria to for instance Serbian or Greek markets.

South Stream will directly have to interact with European gas grids, where Nord Stream does not. Regulatory conditions require large involvements of national authorities in the connected countries, together with the European Commission. South Stream did not (yet) receive the status of a project of European Interest and it is not clear yet what the final criteria for such a status would look like. In addition, there will also be interactions with energy market regulations, where details are determined by the still developing technical characteristics of the project. As an example, in some of the involved smaller Balkan countries, annual capacity options under discussion range from 4 to 20 bcm.

The question ofTPA will be a key issue, pending the final integrated feasibility study of the project. Unclear are also the precise rules coming from the national implementations of the Third package. Especially the question needs to be raised on the exemption clauses and its cross-border impacts, bringing also the role of ACER in the issue, with a further uncertainty. Some would argue that the TPA-issue could be settled when EU companies would be allowed to jointly buy Caspian gas via the CDC (the Caspian Development Cooperation) and shipping this via the Southern gas Corridors, including South Stream. This does as yet not seem to be a realistic avenue, as current understanding on shipping remains that this is just for Gazprom. But it is not be exclude that some larger packages may be thinkable on the project in relation to the broader issue of Caspian Basin gas for the EU.

If the regulatory issues would take some 5 years or so, postponing further the FID, the Southeastern gas market could be developing further, including hubs and other infrastructures and hence South Stream could in the end follow the Nord Stream model and land at the Bulgarian coast with far less regulatory burdens. This is of course contrary to the present project set-up and thinking of the stakeholders which is based on a large onshore section where the national stakeholders will have a 50% stake in their respective national sections. Just landing on the coast does not seem to be realistic as well, as some 60 bcm has to be plugged into the system and expanding the necessary market infrastructure for taking that large amount will not be realized in 5 years time or so.

As a more general issue on the Third package the question arises to what extent a pipeline starting outside the EU jurisdiction would fall under that jurisdiction. There are no precedents for that, as the Norwegian pipelines to the EU are all falling under that jurisdiction and Nord Stream stops at the EU-border but does not enter it. All these regulatory issues are adding to the complexity of the project, require difficult assessments and high-level discussions and decisions. And in the end, there is always the financing question.

1.2.3 The Ukrainian issue

South Stream as it stands gives ground for additional geopolitical and other reflections in relation to the alternatives for bringing gas to the EU via the Southern Corridor. Whereas Nabucco and some other options are focusing on non-Russian supplies and could be considered as "new gas", for South Stream that is less certain. Therefore, it could be seen as a project that would run the risk of drying out existing routes for Russian gas to the EU, i.e. Ukrainian ones. And this perceived overlap of politics and geo-strategy is part of the political discussions. On the other hand, South Stream stakeholders see the project primarily as a business venture, including diversification of supply routes. Upgrading the Ukrainian system needs also major investments in the ranges of several billion euros. And the political and regulatory conditions in that option are not negligible either. They do not see the argument to dry out Ukrainian routes as this route would continue to ship large parts of Russian supplies to the EU anyway.

There is the argument that further supply diversification might lead to a loss of leverage for the Ukraine towards Russia in addition to losing income from transits. This might bring a shift in Ukrainian policy, such as turning "east" again and (re-)integrating into a Russian energy province. This could be a geopolitical concern for the EU, also in gas- terms as Ukraine has very large gas storage capabilities. These facilities could be very important for the Southeastern European market and with the changing role for gas in power generation, also for the electricity market. This brings a challenge to the EU's energy diplomacy, also in relation to Ukraine's membership of the Energy Community Treaty.

Adding pressure on the Ukraine however might be a joint EU-Russia exercise and also be beneficial for the Ukraine in the medium term, as one has to realize that present Income from Ukrainian gas transits is mainly flowing to a small number of interest groups. So a decent and reliable supply route might need to have a break-up of the present system and allow markets and normal business practices to emerge. This would need a joint EU-Russia strategy because we do not want Ukrainian consumers to face gas shortages. This is a further example of the complexities in the question of Ukrainian gas. A question that has its own agenda and specifics, noting that not every project for a LNG-terminal in the region nor even the Nabucco pipeline or other Southern Corridor project are seen by Kiev as a threat to Ukrainian gas transits to EU markets

1.3 Supply routes from the North

Pipeline business from the northern perspective is becoming more and more interesting, also because of the unbundling developments As a business on its own, where shippers have an interest in using it and booking for it, investors are also coming on board. As a nice example, EU traders are seeing opportunities to use the Norwegian transportation system to arbitrage between the UK and the continent. Interactions between that system, the BBL and LNG-imports are adding to market liquidity and requiring new approaches, also regarding system interoperability and integration into the EU. Also from that perspective, Norway sometimes feels itself somewhat underestimated by Brussels, as Norwegian gas, the Norwegian gas system and industry can bring important contributions to the EU gas supply architecture.

Another evolving perspective is the gas-to-electricity balance. Developing oil and sending it to markets is still a one-of-a-kind business. The Norwegian energy ministry is oil and energy. Oil is about exporting oil and gas. Energy is about making money on electricity and having a functioning market. As for gas and its prospects of using it as a flex-fuel in the fuel mix for power generation, a much wider play-of-game would arrive. Power generators are entering that game and are having different criteria than the more conventional gas traders. And since Norway has also large stakes in the hydro-resource basis for the EU power market, some different sums are being made with different outcomes. So for Norway, choices are in the making on where to put the emphasis in the gas-to-power equation.

Gas suppliers, including Norway, are reacting on market signals as well as on policy signals. If, for instance, Brussels is pleading for diversification and flexibility in supplies, suppliers are picking up on that. It will have impacts on the way in which capacity is booked, open seasons are being used, options are created without the need to use them and the various price clauses in the long-term contracts are being explored and even tested. Algerian Sonatrach and Russian Gazprom were also confronted with these market demands and gave clear negative signals. Norwegian reactions were perhaps a little more prudent, being a somewhat more kind of captive producer due to its precision. It all underlines the notion of the way markets are working, emotions are playing a role and policy makers need to take that into account. If the EU wants to establish a sound and secure supply architecture, it has to be part of that game.

1.4 Shale gas

The future EU gas supply situation needs also some consideration as to the role of *shale gas*. Wide prospects may be coming available in continental Europe, and especially in the central and eastern parts of the Union. These prospects have to be faced in a realistic way, understanding that what is happening in the US or elsewhere when CBM (Coal Bed Methane) is involved might not be the model for Europe. Economic and environmental concerns, together with different regulatory regimes, might bring these perspectives in a more realistic mode and could avoid the occurrence of a bubble in unconventional gas deployments. Figure 3 gives a short overview of the European potentials, where the Norwegian resource base should not be underestimated. On the other hand, it may be questionable if Norway would be interested to develop these resources, as they still have many other opportunities to develop. European countries that are gas-importers face a different situation, as it would help them to manage their gas supply basis in a more stable and balanced way. This would also be the case for the UK that has also large coal bed-methane potentials close to markets.

Top 10 European shale gas resources*	Natural gas reserves** (Tcm)	Importers (✔)/ Exporters(✗)	Shale gas resources* (Tcm)	Shale gas production by 2020***
Poland	0.16	✔	5.30	✔
France	0.01	✔	5.10	?
Norway	2.04	✗	2.35	?
Ukraine	1.10	✔	1.19	✔
Sweden	–	✔	1.16	?
Denmark	0.06	✗	0.65	✔
UK	0.25	✔	0.57	✔
Netherlands	1.39	✗	0.48	?
Turkey	0.01	✔	0.42	✔
Germany	0.17	✔	0.23	✔
Others			0.54	

Source: World Shale Gas Resources: An Initial Assessment of 14 Regions Outside the United States, April 2011

* Technically recoverable shale gas resources
** Proved conventional natural gas reserves
*** Sund Energy estimates

Figure 3. Shale and other unconventional gas potentials in Europe

New unconventional gas technologies, other than shale gas, could also play a role, especially when both the vast potentials of hard coal that exist in the EU and the options for biogas or green gas are considered. That could be done via the CBM-technology, but maybe even more so the technologies of underground gasification with power stations on top of them, with innovative carbon sequestration and underground storage or nearby re-use options around them. As to greening the gas on the basis of biomass or biowaste, new roads are being explored, especially in the Netherlands and Germany. If these options would be rewarding to be further explored, they again might have an impact on the infrastructures needed, both in gas transmission and in storage.

1.5 Supply routes and EU market needs

1.5.1 Introduction

EU perceptions of its own role and the need for a different gas supply architecture should consider that the EU share in the global gas market is diminishing. There are many projections on the EU‘s future gas demand and import needs, and these have impacts on investments in transport routes. Figure 4 gives an indication as seen from the South Stream perspective.

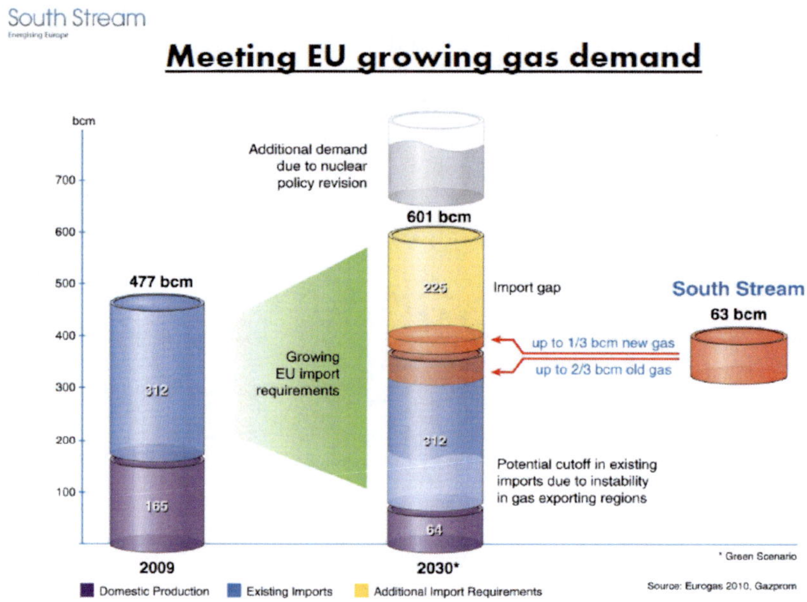

Figure 4. EU gas import needs and options

The rather common expectation that the role of LNG might improve the overall external gas supply base for the EU has to be reconsidered. Although the increased role of LNG-exports to the EU gas market has to be recognized, in the medium to longer term supply situation long-haul pipelines will continue to dominate EU gas-imports, and hence EU-reliance on these infrastructures. The EU's gas import needs for the post 2030 period, when the energy system is expected to be less carbon-based, could raise issues around market prospects for investments in supply routes with lifetimes expanding largely beyond that year. The long-term demand projection for imported gas to the EU remains a strong one, especially as a fuel for power generation. With all the uncertainties about renewables, coal and nuclear, gas remains a preferred choice and/or a choice of consequence.

1.5.2 Changing market conditions?

Changing risk sharing mechanisms in long-term supply contracts is the next challenge. Traditionally, LTC's were the preferred risk-sharing coordination mechanisms throughout the supply chain, especially when new and major upstream investments were required. However, with the increased role of shorter term market mechanisms in the further liberalizing internal EU-market, the impact of spot-pricing is set to increase. This will have various impacts, not least on the price indexation formulae in the LTC's, but also on the role of oil price indexation clauses. This, in itself, might have a backlash on the attractiveness of EU markets for the external suppliers.

A major driver might be the role of gas in the changing fuel mix for power generation. With the increasing role of intermittent energy sources and the need for balancing and backing-up the electricity system, gas as a flexible deliverable and relatively clean fossil fuel and also with relatively easy and cheap possibilities of expanding gas-fired power generation installations, might create for itself a new "golden era". In order to meet these challenged opportunities, the gas business has to explore and introduce much more short-term oriented and flexible business arrangements. And that would include pricing formulas that would go beyond the question of oil. Spot-term based pricing may be one answer, allowing also efficient usage of balancing markets, but more electricity oriented pricing may be another one, where also on the day pricing could play a role. A further price reference could be found in the carbon market, where carbon-prices will be a critical factor in determining day-to-day gas (and coal) use in power generation.

These elements could be very relevant for suppliers, where some tend to go for maximizing value where others may choose for volume. The first one could seem to be more appropriate in a flex-fuel context than the latter one. Similar consequences might come up however when the infrastructure services and their pricing and tarification formulas might be considered, including issues around the business incentives for investing in (additional) back-up capacities for power generation. As a final reflection on these developments, suppliers might seek new opportunities by entering further downstream into the EU market, seeking opportunities in increasing their commodity values, for instance, by entering the power generating market. This is already happening in the German market, where the nuclear phase-out policy is bringing new challenges for the gas industry. Therefore, if the EU-market wants to continue to be attractive for external gas suppliers new business models might bring further add-ons to this position.

Bringing gas from abroad to European gas markets therefore needs also some thinking about gas pricing strategies. It is not only a question of continuing oil price indexed long-term contracts or not, or relying more or less on spot market indicators, but it is also a more fundamental question that might come up and that is about the position that gas will take in the market and it's developing contributions to wider fuel mix considerations. Are suppliers able and willing to consider more innovative approaches, are consumers strong enough to require them. The history of the gas business has seen some innovative thinking and experiments, especially in European gas theatres. A rethinking of a new architecture for securing European gas supplies might not hide away from this.

1.5.3 Some reflections on the EU's external gas supply relations

The EU has consumer power, it is a very large and mature gas market where consumers are increasingly adding their voice, their preferences and their quality demands. Effective energy diplomacy should try to use these powers in an intelligent way, bringing these powers to the forefront and lining up the EU's gas supply businesses. This will become more pertinent in the global setting where the EU will face competitive conditions with suppliers and with other importing consumers. Some of these consumers are organized in a very effective way, using mechanisms that are intelligently bringing consumer power to the front. China and other emerging markets need to be mentioned in this regard.

Developing and focusing the EU's external gas supply policy, the EU-Russia dimension will remain the priority issue. However, relations are loaded, or maybe even saturated, with politics and sometimes irrational dimensions. Part of that comes from the large differences within the EU with regards to gas import dependency from Russia. Most central and eastern EU member states are considering the Russian gas case as part of their supply security problems, whereas present and future gas importing member states on the EU's western borders consider Russian gas as part of the solution. The other part comes from the EU-idea that the prevailing EU liberalized market model needs to be exported to the East as well. Past and ongoing discussions on gas industry structures, such as the ownership unbundling of infrastructures, gas market designs, and the target model, are not always helpful in building and developing a secure gas supply system between the EU and Russia. A further complication comes from the EU's policy towards the Caspian Basin and its Southern Gas Corridors.

Although it has to be recognized that so far the EU has not been able to develop a coherent external energy supply policy, the EU's track-record on energy diplomacy has not always been helpful either. But, no doubt again, priority focus needs to be given to the EU-Russia dimension with its do's and don'ts of a smart diplomacy. It should help the EU to consider and formulate in a more precise the way the strategic political choices it has to make in this respect. Questions could be raised about the relation between the energy and other dossiers that are part of the EU-Russia agenda, including the wider implications of the more general framework of the EU-Russia Partnership Agreement. The new focus on strengthening the EU-Russia Energy Dialogue could be helpful in this respect, with its more specific formulation of a number of issues to be tackled. The two sides however have to make this dialogue really a dialogue.

Smarter energy diplomacy for EU-MENA relations could on the other hand be done in a broader way than just on gas, or even expanding on the energy question in general. The EU could possibly expand its use of soft power, seeking wider cooperation in the Mediterranean and Gulf Cooperation frameworks. Win-win situations in terms of energy projects, both in gas and in renewable energies such as CSP (Concentrated Solar Power) and understanding the region's basic needs and interests, could add to further stability in the region. The EU already has a number of institutional frameworks that could prove to be effective in this regard, such as the MEDREG cooperation and the proposals to enhance interconnections in gas and in electricity. On the other hand, realism should prevail with projects like Desertec should serve as a warning, bringing major technological and financial risks and even bringing the risk of deterioration of relationships.

1.5.4 The EU external/internal policy balance

It might be seen as a desirable approach to include energy market liberalization as a policy objective in the context of the EU Neighborhood Policy. It could however also be quite productive to approach some of the EU's bordering states on a more specific case-by-case basis, taking into account the various individual circumstances in their national energy market concepts and structures. An additional featured dilemma of this balance would be the issue of framing contractual relations between the EU gas industry and its external suppliers. Around the ongoing discussions with the suppliers bordering the Caspian Sea, ideas are floating on the formation of gas purchasing consortia or even in a wider sense on that of an EU Gas Supply Agency. The internal market rules for competition might create legal and political obstacles, but signals from some of those suppliers would be a challenge to find smart solutions for win-win mechanisms for future gas supplies. In that context the mandate for the EU Commission to negotiate the conditions for building a Trans Caspian Pipeline might prove to be an opportunity to new suppliers if not a serious challenge to established gas exporters such as Russia.

On the more general internal market perspective, the discussions on EU gas market designs and target models should give due account of the potential impact on external supplier's perspectives. Suppliers have legitimate interests on issues such as bringing gas not only to EU markets but also through EU markets to final destinations. The rule to introduce entry-exit tariffs for transmission is another one, together with the conditions for the participation non-EU industries in the TSO's.

1.6 A final reflection on global gas supplies

The position of the EU in the developing global gas markets is not always approached in a realistic way. Generally speaking, government officials and politicians within the EU tend to be overly optimistic with respect to external gas supply diversification prospects. Not only do the prospects of the EU's call on global LNG supplies tend to be overstated, the prospects of bringing non-Russian gas supplies via new pipelines to EU markets are also not always realistically assessed. Again, energy diplomacy is not only an art for Brussels and national capitals alike, but it also needs a coherent view on the role of gas in the longer-term EU energy mix, and a clear strategy with a set of internal arrangements that would allow a coherent EU to sing the same songs to the outside world. The prevailing opportunities and the political choices for the EU and its strategic approaches to its external gas suppliers need to include clearly expressed external signals and messages at the right political levels. These signals need to be more innovative in the sense that smart energy diplomacies could cover win-win energy -and other projects-for the Mediterranean basin, could be more open and flexible when discussions are taking place with neighboring countries on their respective energy market structures, and finally could be more direct in its dealings with the EU's major suppliers on the wider balance between supply security and demand security. As to the Union's own role in relation to the roles of national capitals, a smarter use could be made of the precedents coming from the external trade procedures, where the

Union is responsible for the regulatory external trade frameworks and national capitals taking the lead for the promotion of using these frameworks. The new Commission Communication on external energy policy[4] might provide new opportunities for enhancing the discussions on these issues.

2. The challenges for EU infrastructures

2.1 Gas infrastructures

ENTSO-G is the organization that is representing the EU's gas transmission system operators. Membership of ENTSOG is mandatory for all TSO's and it still remains to be seen how many of those will be going through the certification procedure under the 3rd Package. For ENTSO-G it is quite clear that developing gas-infrastructure is first of all driven by energy policy with its policy objectives and dilemmas regarding sustainability, security and competition. Gas demand is affected largely by these policies, but also by the way in which the gas market is integrating. New supplies will be necessary to meet new demand, leading to new cross-border gas flows and new infrastructures. These will have to manage new imports, as domestic production in the EU is declining. In addition, due to the expanding role for renewable energy sources and the potential of gas as a backup fuel, gas needs to become more and more flexible. This will further influence system designs and operations together with access arrangements.

There are many technological drivers in this process, both on the demand side and demand structure, but also on the way in which gas is transported and the system is operated. On the demand side, new mobility solutions such as natural gas vehicles or LNG for heavy transport shipping are being seen. The new Security of Supply Regulation with its requirement to apply the N-1 rule, the drive to increase cross-border trade and competition, they need to bring innovative designs for managing congestions in the system and the adaptation of balancing rules. With respect to transport itself for instance, excess power from renewable energy could be is stored as hydrogen or when CO_2 is transformed into methane, both gases could be put back on the grids.

4 Communication from the Commission On security of energy supply and international cooperation; "The EU Energy Policy": Engaging with Partners beyond Our Borders; COM/2011/0539 final Brussels 7 September 2011.

And again, new investments are necessary, with new solutions and new technological devices.

The political ambitions to move this to a fully integrated single gas market in Europe is adding to this infrastructure challenge. As yet, the situation still exists where most member states have a very strong national focus and national objectives. And this impacts the regulatory designs and the regulatory discussions. One element would be the discussion on the number of entry-exit zones. One needs to realize that an increase of the size of an entry/exit zone probably requires also more capacity because it is uncertain to know in advance to what extends this will cause changing gas flows. The larger the zone, the greater the number of constraints in the system and the more balancing instruments will be needed. Increasing the size of the entry/exit zones has advantages, but obviously comes at the price of dealing with these constraints. It could also cause undesirable cross-subsidies and socialization, which are not reflective of the shippers' use of the system. Furthermore, if an entry/exit zone would encompass more than one Member State, it would require substantial cooperation and harmonization amongst TSOs, but also amongst regulators. This is part of the discussion on the Gas Target Model. But before these issues are tackled, it would be necessary to define the kind of network the EU would need. What are the objectives for further developments, also in terms of resilience to external supply shocks? And this means some kind of infrastructure planning.

ENTSOG's contribution to the debate about the infrastructure challenge is to develop, under the 3rd Package, the 10 Year Network Development Plan. This 10YNDP aims to offer a pan-European view on the supply-demand and capacity developments and the resulting needs for new investments. It should take due account of the wider gas market dynamics. A new 10YNDP was published in 2011, containing information about projects with and without a final investment decision (FID), divided into underground storages (UGS), pipelines and LNG-terminals. Figure 5 gives an overview, indicating a total investment of some € 100 billion. For some projects the FID will be negative and will not take place, some are still indicative and for some others information was not always quite clear, therefore costs may even be on the low side. Anyway, the amounts are quite large and hence it's a big challenge for the TSOs. It is also an indication that project sponsors are rather confident that the investments will pay themselves out in the long term, so they must have a positive outlook of the EU gas market.

UGS	FID	Non-FID	Pipes	FID	Non-FID	LNG	FID	Non-FID
Projects	26	22	Projects	62	97	Projects	11	20
10^6 €	4260	2593	10^6 €	13711	58556	10^6 €	3570	6614

Figure 5. Planned investments in EU gas infrastructures (ENTSO-G 10YNDP)

The overview is based on inputs from the TSO's themselves. This is only part of the story. The other input comes from the global design base of the network with its interactions between network users, shippers, traders, suppliers and TSOs. This is the story of physical realities, market functioning and market needs, where the need for sustaining supply security and system reliability may make it worthwhile having more infrastructure capacity than needed on the basis of a theoretical model. There are limits of course, but a relevant consideration would be that the costs of infrastructure as part of the end user bill are generally in the order of 4%. So it's better to err on the high side than on the low side. Then there is also the role of storage, where through the modeling of the 10YNDP it was found that in the high demand scenarios more storage is really important. It might even go beyond what is currently planned in FID's.

Figure 6 gives an overview of all the potential bottlenecks under certain scenario's that might need to get further attention and eventually even more investments. This capacity map from the 10YNDP is also based on inputs from producers and suppliers and is translated into a commercial simulation model, simulating different flows under different assumptions. The message would be that there are still a number of potential bottlenecks in the system, for instance in NW Europe and in Central Europe, that need to be addressed. The message underlies further the relevance of a sound investment framework as a very important feature for the entire EU gas market. Scarcity of infrastructure is something that can be very detrimental and may lead to higher bills for end consumers. The regulatory framework for giving the right incentives for investments in infrastructure is therefore a condition sine qua non for the entire EU gas market.

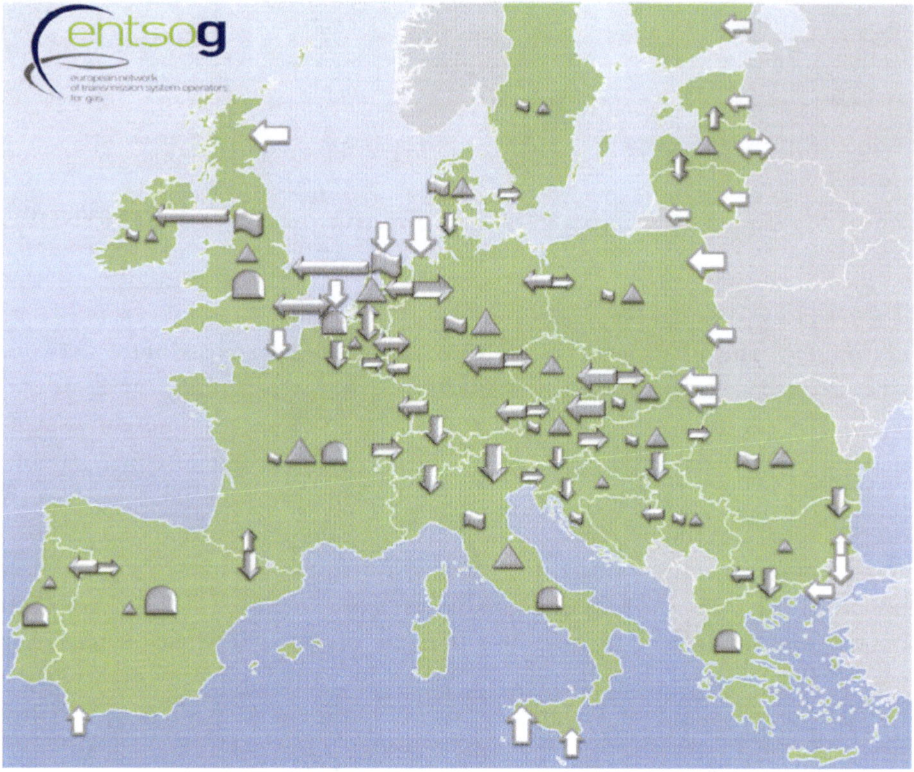

Figure 6. Infrastructure capacity bottlenecks; ENTSO-G 10YNDP

Regulatory design that is still being further developed in the EU needs to take full account of the dynamic environment that markets are bringing. The unbundling processes emerging from the 3rd Package is getting into a high gear, where all TSOs are looking at their options. From those that have not ownership unbundled or are not choosing to do so, some may go the ISO-route, whereas others may opt for the ITO. It could be questioned whether these choices are sustainable in the long run. Many observers are of the opinion that transmission will become more and more independent of production and supply interests. And if this trend to full independence continues, it may mean less requirements for strict and detailed ex ante regulatory rules. The consolidation that is going on between the TSOs is moving in the direction of further inter-TSO-cooperation and integrating market areas, which are also largely driven by the unbundling process. More TSO-independence should therefore require fewer rules. There is however a tendency that the ex-ante regulatory system is further expanding and becoming a "business-of-its-own".

It would be useful to further reflect on this in the context of allowing markets to work properly and to limit regulatory intervention only when necessary.

Allowing markets to work is also related to level playing fields and preventing market distortions in infrastructure. There is no doubt that tens of billions of Euros have to be invested in gas-infrastructures. And this is a role for markets, with government intervention to be kept to a minimum and only when really needed. The discussion at EU-levels tends to go in the opposite direction, with a strong focus on central planning and even a stronger one on EU-funding. The lessons from the EU's Economic Recovery Program are apparently not being learned, where projects were publicly funded that were competing with projects funded by the market. The new proposed facility under the Connecting Europe program, with its amount of some € 9 billion for energy infrastructure, tends to go in the same direction. In addition, the 3rd Package gave also the NRAs a wider mandate and a stronger independence, maybe leading to a stronger focus on national interests without too much concern for the wider EU interest of integrating gas markets. This might also inhibit investments decisions for infrastructures, especially when EU funds become available for which the national interests per definition tend to compete with each other. Sub-optimal outcomes may be the result, not always meeting consumer benefits.

2.2 The role of gas storage

This role is enhanced [5] with the Dutch Bergermeer project from Taqa Energy as an example. Especially taking into account the EU's decreasing domestic gas production versus increasing market needs, external gas supplies will become more important. And they are basically long-haul ones and hence are not able to adjust supply-demand balances at shorter terms. They do not work as a "click-on-the-button". There are thus increasing opportunities for expanding gas storages, also when the role of gas as a flexible fuel for meeting the intermittency challenge in power generation is taken into account. Figure 7 gives an indication of developments in storage projects in the NW European region. They all have different perspectives and planning horizons. The Bergermeer one, once in operation, will become the biggest open access gas storage project in Europe. It will be almost doubling the existing storage

5 See also: "Seasonal Flexibility in the Northwest European Gas Market. An Outlook for 2015 and 2020", Energy Paper. Clingendael International Energy Programme (April 2011).

capacity in the Netherlands, and there may be another need for a similar project by 2020 based on some market assumptions.

The Bergermeer however has a wider functioning potential than just the Dutch market. It may also play a role for the UK market, where up to now only some 5% of the demand is covered by storage. That role may become even more important when gas-flows through Nord Stream will become available for the NW-European market, especially since Taqa entered into a partnership with Gazprom. Gazprom will supply all the cushion gas that is needed in return for a share of the working volume, so they are seeing the Bergermeer as one of the end points to Nord Stream. But next to Nord Stream there is more gas coming to the area, gas from north to south, from Norway to Spain, from east to west through Nordstream and other pipelines towards the UK. Gas is also coming through the LNG-terminals, including the new Gate terminal at Rotterdam. And this is all adding to market activity, where gas traded on the Dutch TTF is further increasing as well.

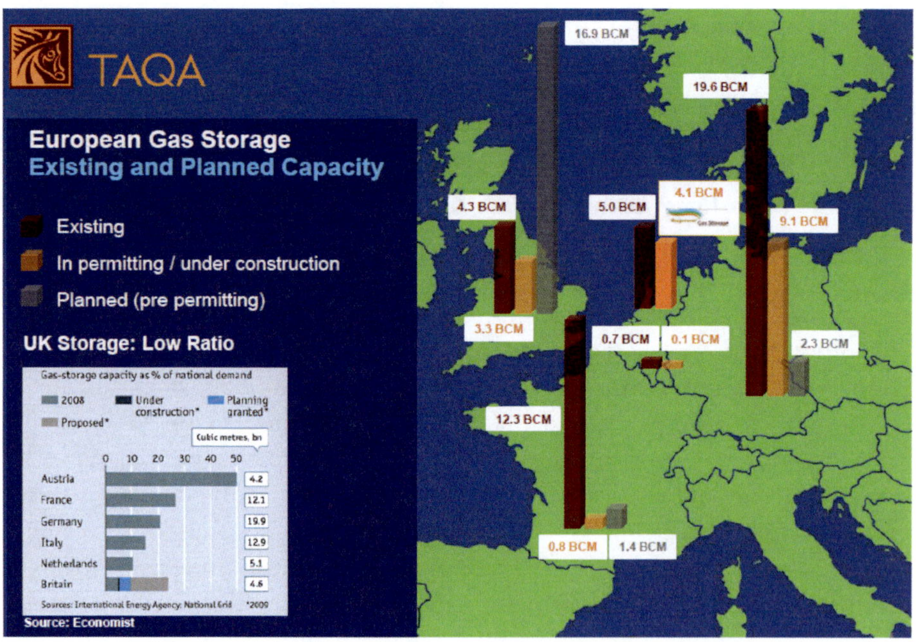

Figure 7. Gas Storages in NW-Europe

It is quite clear that Bergermeer is a major investment project, not only covering an initial amount of some € 800 million, but as a commitment is given of a ten year capacity period, total investment for building and operating the project comes to some € 3 billion. And this brings us to the regulatory environment and the regulatory risks. One important feature is the uncertainty about the transmission tariffs for bringing the gas to and from Bergermeer. This would also require expanding pipeline capacity by GTS, the Dutch TSO. Discussions are still ongoing, but final conclusions are still pending. Uncertainty on the access to the storage seems to be settled as the Dutch government has concluded that negotiated TPA is the rule, meaning no ex ante regulatory intervention.

Uncertainty on the project still exists on the permitting front, where thirteen authorities are involved, including several municipalities. For one of them, near the facility, NIMBY is the leading issue, and final appeal procedures are still not settled. There is however a general belief that the permitting issue will be settled in a positive outcome for the project. Once a further safety investigation mandated by the Dutch Council of State has been completed and the final decision is taken (expected early 2012), commercial operation could start by 2014. Bergermeer therefore, as a major European storage project in a country with a lot of interests in the gas business, is also dependent on difficult regulatory procedures that per definition are adding to uncertainties and are requiring quite some patience of its stakeholders.

2.3 Specific considerations

A number of more specific considerations are to be added to the more general reflections on the infrastructure challenge. Issues such as financing, market designs and capacity bookings and markets, regulatory risks, the role of national regulators and their relation with the new ACER and finally, regulatory designs and market dynamics.

2.3.1 Financing new infrastructure

The issue is always where to find the money and what are the right conditions. When for instance a TSO needs to expand its capacity due to the regulatory requirement, such as coming from the 10YNDP, it may have no money to fund this, or no shareholder to raise that money. As the 3rd package seems to be indicating, tendering by third parties may be another option, even in combination with long term leases to the TSO concerned. A further option may be coming from new capital from pension funds and other institutional capital funds that are seeking relatively risk-free and stable outlets for their capital. But, the situation may be very different for the various TSO's, depending also on their organizational set-ups and their degrees of ownership unbundling structures. Public funding is also mentioned some times, but it would bring additional political interference and processes. And, although many MSs may have their doubts, when this is done at EU-level on the basis of an EU facility, every capital will lobby for a share, and this might then lead to sub-optimal results in the end.

Financing new investments will also be influenced by the structure of the TSO-industry, with questions around ownership and the implementation of the 3rd package rules. As ISOs will not happen in gas and the ITO could be only a transitional option, at the end of the day all TSOs may be fully independent and ownership unbundled. This could be a lengthy process, but developments could be overtaken by what is happening on the market side. As there will be more and more cross-border cooperation needed, a further consolidation of TSOs and market areas will follow. These developments will really force NRAs and national governments to deal with regulatory frameworks, necessary to facilitate that. If however TSO-owners would still choose today for an ITO, they will probably do so as they would expect not be able to raise enough money from selling their network assets. Going the ITO-route with its detailed regulatory set-ups would mean no control and no rights over the assets as in the case of the integrated company. Capital will be tied up with relatively modest returns compared to commercial business. Shareholders will not be happy with that, leading to unstable models bringing full ownership unbundling rather sooner than later.

2.3.2 Market designs and capacity markets

Tariffs and their cost bases is one thing, other elements may be as relevant when new investments will have to be made. A clear distinction has to be made between the commodity part of the business and the capacity part, i.e. the capacity for transmission. There is quite some progress towards more integrated commodities markets, with all sorts of impacts on the gas trade as well, but not so much on capacity markets. There may be evolving a need for some platform or some process through which bidding and booking for capacity in a coordinated way could be arranged for. It would be useful to make a distinction between existing and new capacity. In particular, the forthcoming rules on capacity allocation management that require 10% of capacity to be kept free for short-term allocation at later points in time are to be mentioned. This 10 percent can be very useful for short-term market considerations and be very relevant for shippers. In some circumstances it could even be sold several times over and be quite profitable. Especially when there is something like a limitation of re-nomination rights, some of that short term capacity could be very necessary. An important feature however would be the determination of the reserve price. And as yet, this feature is not properly addressed and is lacking in the ongoing consultation processes on the codes and guidelines. It is also very much interlinked with the other features in capacity allocation, such as the role of auctioning. It may be essential for this piece of the puzzle to be somehow slotted in.

TSOs are anyway under obligation to develop their network under economic conditions. If 90 percent of the new capacity is contracted for the long term and 10 percent is not, it may make the decision a little more difficult. For most TSOs the need that a significant portion of the capacity is covered by long term contracts probably will do. The 10 percent "free capacity" could, as indicated, be profitable as well but it brings anyway some additional risk. A side effect may be that shippers will count on the availability of always 10 percent free capacity, and hence refrain from booking this capacity in advance. On the 90 percent share, open seasons for assessing shipper interests in new capacity will probably be the way to go. Especially when new investments are needed in a cross-border context, some form of coordinated procedures would then be very relevant. This could be done via coordinated open-seasons, but however they are as yet usually taking place on a case-by-case basis, although these cross-border investments would be quite relevant for combining intra-EU gas flows. As an example, there is an EU priority to have a north-south corridor in Eastern Europe for security of supply purposes. But the open season to connect Slovakia and Hungary is taking place on one day, and the one between the Czech Republic and Poland on another day. And even the ones covering other flows such as between Denmark/Poland, Sweden and Norway, are not part of these procedures. So there is a need for some platform where all these procedures are put together. It may be complex to arrive at this, especially when also auctioning is included. Some of the UK lessons on the role of auctioning may be relevant, in order to preserve the paradigm of a market-driven system instead of falling back to an old style market involving transit.

It may be forward looking but the process of developing the new EU network codes would put ENTSO-G in a strong position to make relevant proposals for these issues, and it would then be hard for the European Commission not to back them. It would also give a clear format for deciding on new transmission lines, further enhancing the options for long term capacity rights. It could create a regular process in canvassing the needs for cross-border capacities. The more such a process would be expanded on a regional basis, the more a real capacity market might be evolving, even a long term capacity market. It could facilitate the challenge to provide the relevant forward-looking investment signals and would be able to underpin the long term commitments that will be necessary to add to long term supply security arrangements.

2.3.3 Risks associated with energy policy and energy regulation

Whereas so far issues were mentioned that are more or less coming from within the TSO-industry, even more relevant features are coming from the global environment they are working in. Surveys and other regular overviews of business perspectives about the risk factors of the energy industry mention as the number one risk issue the regulatory risk. Examples are numerous, but it is the new world that the energy industry is living in, whether regulated or not. In the EU the 3rd package and its implementation, together with REMIT, and forthcoming more general regulations, such as EMIR and MIFID, have major impacts on the energy industry. This is also putting major strains on the NRA's and their respective governments, and they will have to find the right balance between the market and the regulation. In this balance regulators should not only try to limit the cost of compliance and of doing business but aim for a transparent and sound regulatory design that is serving the overall public interest. In other words: go for smart regulation.

In this whole context, the role of regulatory authorities cannot be underestimated. The NRA-TSO interaction in many countries is still under development, as most of the NRA's have a relatively young lifespan. This does not only apply to the NRA's as they are, but also in relation to the new Agency, ACER, that has a particular mandate to promote and facilitate inter-NRA cooperation, especially when there are cross-border impacts. One has to be aware however that not only ACER has no role in "steering" the NRAs, also ministries and other political institutions have only limited possibilities for intervention in NRA-decision making. Most NRAs have in many cases quite some large mandates and a strong independency in applying these. Although there are always procedures for appeal to specific courts, but most courts tend to focus on the procedural environment of the NRA-decisions and less on the substance matters. The same would apply for the interactions between NRAs and their national governments. In some MSs, the choice was made to attach the energy regulator to other regulatory bodies, or even to merge them with competition authorities[6]. This last point could also be part of the philosophy to use "markets were possible and governments and regulation only when necessary". A regulatory body that is embodied into a competition authority would have the incentive to act accordingly.

A key element for instance in the discussion on investments in new infrastructures is the allowed rate of return and the resulting translation into transmission tariffs and their base in tariff structures. NRAs are the determining institutions, based on the national rules coming from the implementation of the 3rd package. And these national rules are related to the more general financial and fiscal regulations with their impacts as well on the financial conditions for new infrastructures. But when cross-border issues are involved, some harmonization of structures and tariff-settings may be very relevant for the investment decisions, and up to now it is unclear whether ACER will be able to play a role in this regard.

The NRA-ACER interaction is still developing and finding a way out how to comply with or even manage the national mandates of the NRAs. This is very different from the US situation where interstate pipelines are regulated by FERC, the Federal Energy Regulatory Commission. But the EU is not the US and one should accept that the ACER-NRA process is just beginning. It will be a very critical one as most, if not all, of the major investments in new infrastructure in the gas market, will have a cross-border or a cross-national interest. A mechanism is needed for facilitating inter NRA-cooperation on bilateral or even tri- or multilateral levels and solving outstanding issues on which NRAs would fail to agree on. That is a primary role for ACER, as it would secure wider regional market interests and even an all-EU one. It's a first step for ACER to deliver. And it can be done within the 3rd package, not needing a 4th one. The Commission proposal for a regulation on guidelines for trans-European energy infrastructure gives further guidance and possibilities for ACER to act.

---

6 Reference could be made to the situations in the Netherlands and in Denmark.

On another philosophical note regarding regulatory design and market dynamics, the balance between regulatory stability and market dynamics could be mentioned. This is an ongoing quest in many areas. Are NRAs able to react to a dynamic market development as it is the environment in which the regulated entity is working in, usually asking for a quick response? But when the NRA is tied to a too much specified regulatory mandate, creative solutions in giving quick responses are usually not possible. This would call for a very general mandate with some global objectives, including the ones on sustainability and supply security. It would allow the NRA to find a balance between its traditional task to enhance competitiveness and efficiency in line with the evolving market dynamics and policy agendas. It would also help NRAs to focus more on a process of effective stakeholder involvement and participation and less on the more detailed outcome. The NRAs have the task to organize the process very well and allow market parties to participate in that process. Open seasons or platforms for capacity allocations might be perfect examples in order to do that. NRAs would be able to focus more on managing and securing a process that would bring all the relevant interests on the table in order to secure a fair outcome.

A special note needs to be given in this context on the EU's external suppliers. Realizing that they need to invest large amounts of money to develop production and supply lines that EU consumers would like to be served with, suppliers such as Gazprom and Qatar Petroleum are complaining about understanding the EU market and its governance by a variety of countries and authorities that may even be working in different directions. It's not only the supplier company as such, but more important their share holders. As they are large investors, such as for instance the Abu Dhabi sovereign wealth fund that owns Taqa, the large storage company, they are quite able to redirect their investments to different countries or continents if they perceive the risks as too high. It's not always easy to explain to them the European story. EU institutions, industry and regulators should raise their efforts to make this story a successful one.

2.4 A final reflection on the challenges

A number of bottle-necks when it comes to new investments in infrastructure, securing longer term supply security in gas still exist. Financing is a key to the solution and the best condition for that is by many regarded as the one of a well-functioning market that would provide the best guarantee for security of supply. A well-functioning market has more dimensions than just security of supply as it is also essential for the promotion of competition and for the sustainability objectives. For the market there are many good reasons to invest into the infrastructure that is needed to get facilitate this market. There are however always situations where the market will not be able or willing to invest. The case of Southeast Europe may be an example, partly due to the very different development phases in relation to the Northwest European example. In these cases some public money could actually help to break through and advance the region further towards the development of the market. This would make the region getting better connected to the other regions in the EU, thereby achieving a better functioning market and also getting the necessary security of supply. But it should continue to be underlined that a sound investment climate, be it for private or for public money is perhaps the most single important condition. And this brings us more in particular to the broader issue of the regulatory challenge in a more generic way.

3. The regulatory challenge

The broader issue of the regulatory framework and its designs, as laid out in a legal set of rules and regulations and its further implementing framework in secondary and tertiary pieces and documents, could be approached in a rather general way, covering the whole value chain as it is effective within the EU, but also from the perspective of the global view about the market concept the EU must be developing to. A concept as a "point-on-the-horizon", guiding the whole implementing process of the 3rd Package. In EU gas market jargon, a Gas Target Model, the GTM. Before moving into that issue, the broader aspects of regulating gas markets is addressed, especially in relation to gas supply security, the main subject of this project.

3.1 Regulating gas

Broadly speaking, the role of regulators is not the central one when referring to security of supply. Other things, such as energy policy, the choice for markets in liberalization, international relations, environmental policy, competition policy, are much more important. One could even argue that the EU Sector Inquiry has had a bigger impact on gas markets than the regulatory process. But it goes without saying that the 3rd package does create a process that is bringing a new regulatory architecture. We now have ENTSO-G, which is not a trade association but a statutory body, we have ACER, another new statutory body and the two of them are instrumental for the network codes that will be put into place. That will take time, but it will eventually become a new regulatory architecture which will define to a large extent how cross border markets in the EU will work. However, one has to make a distinction between regulatory policy, which is not made by regulators but by governments, and its implementation which is largely the job for regulators. The other distinction is to be made between regulation of infrastructure, such as setting tariffs and access rules and investment incentives, and setting rules for the market. On these issues, the infrastructure part of what regulators do is more important for EU gas security of supply.

3.1.1 Infrastructures

Taking the role regulators have in infrastructure, the 3rd package is clear in saying that the NRAs decide on the tariffs that pipelines can charge, and setting methodologies and tariffs also means deciding around the investment decisions by the pipelines. A rather extreme model could be that NRAs require the pipelines to sell capacity on a short term basis only, and if TSOs want to build new capacity, they will approach the NRAs and they will agree to it or not on the basis of regulatory guarantees. That seems to involve a large degree of central planning by the NRA. An alternative approach is the one practiced in Britain and is apparently also the preferred route for ENTSO-G. This approach is to rely on a mix of market signals and central decisions, using for instance "open seasons". In the UK that is dressed up as an auction, with investor incentives. A market based approach that gives incentives to build is probably one of the single biggest things that regulators can do. An important point to make is that the TSO might want to build more than what it gets on the basis of market signals. The UK rule is that if the TSO has a project to build new entry capacity, they need to get market signals which cover half of the cost of doing that. The logic is not only to build for today's users, but also for the ones that will come along in the future. There is another logic that competition requires to have more infrastructure than central planning does, allowing competing suppliers from other sources, hence also adding to security of supply. The balance will come between the interests of the consumer who does not want to fund enormous amounts of infrastructure and the interests of competition and security of supply.

The more centrally organized planning approach is the one where it is accepted to build anyway on the basis of overcapacity at a socialized cost allowing suppliers to come in from everywhere. These two approaches could be highlighted by the experiences in the UK and in Spain when building infrastructures and terminals for LNG. In Spain, the NRA and its government accepted to build terminals with regulated access and tariffs, with costs that were socialized. It brought additional costs for consumers, but also benefits for the country. As a result they have today a market of about 35 bcm, with about 20 bcm of import pipe capacity, and some 60 bcm of LNG import capacity. So this is clearly good for security of supply and the potential to become an LNG hub with all sorts of market advantages.

The UK approach is illustrated by Figure 8, showing UK gas import deliverability. The UK with its around 100 bcm gas market was fully self-sufficient in 2002-2003, including some 20 bcm import capacity. But it was also facing the potential for rapid decline in domestic production. The choice was to go for TPA exemptions under the Gas Directive and the case to proof that this was good for markets and competition and for supply security was broadly and widely accepted. Of course it had to be added that the UK was a liquid market and a hub, attractive for gas suppliers. The result was an expansion in import capacity, with new LNG terminals and new interconnectors, all being exempted and done at the risk of the investors. That was not only fair to the consumer but it would force investors to make good decisions about what infrastructure to build. In 2011 there is now 130 bcm in import capacity, with domestic production still running at some 50 bcm.

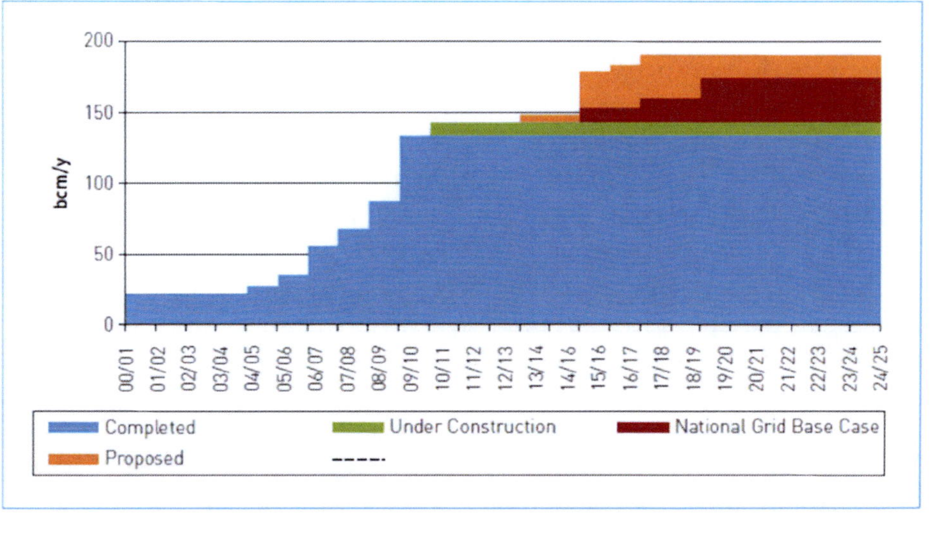

Figure 8. UK Gas Import Capacity (National Grid September 2011)

So the UK and Spain seem to be well positioned in terms of gas-receiving infrastructure and that is good for security of supply. Regulators and policies do have an important role in ensuring that security of supply is going forwards and one way or another, they should give incentives to ensure that "plenty" of infrastructures get built. Although it is a balance, it is better to be on the high side than on the low one. However, it comes at a cost, which is either fully socialized as in Spain, or is based on clear market orientation as in the UK. Both approaches seem to be consistent with liberalization and the vision behind the EU Gas Directive. The two onshore transmission systems are close to consumers and are rather meshed, regulated monopolies. On the upstream side infrastructure is more contestable, especially in the UK, where LNG terminals, interconnectors and storage sites are all competing with each other in bringing gas and flexibility. Since they compete they don't need to be regulated and are part of the competitive landscape. This can be done as the market is reasonably mature and different supply routes and options are possible. This is not the case in many continental EU markets, where markets are much more bound by single supply options and geographical conditions are (as yet) prohibiting efficient and effective alternative supply routings.

3.1.2 Regulating the market?

Regulatory policy on markets should be one of modesty, as markets need to be competitive and competition to be the main discipline. But it cannot be denied that regulators have to act sometimes in a direct way, especially when it comes to setting prices and controlling them in order to protect end consumers. Most experts would disagree with such approaches, but it cannot be denied that governments sometimes require this for political purposes, as household consumers are always voters. It is obvious that when prices are set too low, security of supply would be threatened in general. Two other challenges exist for regulators. One is around the sort of detail of market rules, such as the arrangements defining cross border trade in the internal market. The other one is around emergency situations, when there is a real imminent gas shortage. It is not always quite clear what triggers emergency situations. For instance if there is a very cold winter or when there is default supplier, some countries have the rule that in these cases the TSO needs to step in, on the basis of a number of specific conditions, such as on prices or on duration. Another possibility would exist when there would be a real national emergency. Then strategic stock could be set in, but here again, there is the risk that regulators (or their governments) are tempted to use it for other things like keeping prices down[7]. If they are going to do that, it would mean that the private incentive to invest, to provide peak gas is weakened. Such a measure should only be considered as a final resort. In the case of an emergency that has cross-border implications, there is now the EU Regulation for Supply Security. It is not only putting the obligation on MSs to have a number of emergency measures in place, but also requires EU-wide coordination of actions, where also ACER has to play its role.

3.2 The Gas Target Model

The issue of defining a Gas Target Model (GTM) received much attention of all stakeholders and was heavily debated in the course of 2011. Basis for the discussion was the request formulated at the meeting of the 18th Madrid Forum (December 2010), where the Commission and the regulators were invited to

"*explore, in close cooperation with system operators and other stakeholders, the interaction and interdependence of all relevant areas for network codes and to initiate a process establishing a gas market target model*".

The desired target model should have as its purpose to provide a unifying vision on the future layout of the European gas market architecture. That vision should assist all stakeholders in quickly and efficiently implementing the 3rd energy market package on the internal gas market in a consistent way. It is also supposed to prevent inconsistencies in developing the Framework Guidelines for the EU Network Codes. This brought a number of ideas that were put on the table by think-tanks and consultants, using acronyms such as ASCOS, EURAM or MECOS [8].

In this chapter the focus on the GTM-discussion will be put on the process of formulating a Gas Target Model and on the further way forward. As to the subject matter and the contents, the CIEP-model will be briefly mentioned together with some of the most debated issues, i.e. the role of wholesale markets

7 The IEA set a precedent in 2011 by deciding on some emergency stock draw-down for influencing oil prices in the market.

8 A Vision for the EU Gas Target Model: The MECOS-model; Jean–Michel Glachant; www.florence-school.eu/portal/page/portal/FSR_HOME/ENERGY/Publications/Working_Papers/2011/RSCAS_2011_38.rev.pdf ; An American model for the EU Gas Market? Sergio Ascari; www.florence-school.eu/portal/page/portal/FSR_HOME/ENERGY/Publications/Working_Papers/2011/RSCAS_2011_39.pdf; CIEP Vision on the Gas Target Model; www.clingendael.nl/publications/2011/20110819_ciep_energypaper_gas_target_model.pdf

and long-term contracts, the options for market merging and interconnection, the capacity allocation and congestion management approaches, the meaning of criteria such as price alignment and market liquidity, the relation with external suppliers and, finally, the broader context of Gas Supply Security, the main theme of this project.

3.2.1 The GTM-process

The whole process had and still has the potential of being one of the most ambitious moves in setting the regulatory framework on the EU Gas Market, with a large impact on the industry. A number of alternative models and ideas have been floating around, creating many misunderstandings that are often due to a lack of discussion. Using different words for the same thing, arguing around with lacks of knowing and or fully understanding the whole market and its value chains, exploring implementations in certain and specific ways with different interpretations. Market coupling as one issue for instance, has to be assessed very carefully, in line with short term congestion, maybe on the basis of specific pilots. Merging entry-exit zones or trading zones clearly have their pros and cons and may need further cost benefit analysis. The German experience in merging their market zones might give some answers, together with the process in Ireland where merging the markets of Northern Ireland and Ireland is on the agenda. Questions will have to be addressed also about the size of the entry/exit zones and their relations with hubs and linking. All these and other issues would require further thinking and discussion.

Many workshops were organized, although not always in a way to bring "the right people" together, or giving them sufficient time (for a week or so) to sort out the relevant issues and concepts. Most of the workshops were organized in a way that presentations were given, where many stakeholders were sitting together, sorting some things out, however without coming to common conclusions. Sometimes these workshops even added more to the confusion than resolving them. Language plays a role, where most participants are forced to use English without being their mother tongue, with also different experiences in these processes between representatives from old and new member states.

The process also did run the risk that too much attention is paid to the idea that markets could be designed by rules and regulations, by laws, by regulators and or governments. That clearly is a mistake as markets are designed by themselves, by market parties, suppliers and producers, consumers and traders. Of course governments and regulators have to set boundary conditions and intervene in markets when market outcomes are not acceptable. Precedents and models coming from the electricity sector were maybe getting too much attention, focus and relevance for gas, with the issue of market coupling being a good example. Gas molecules are gas molecules, without a passport and when they come from Russia, entering the EU market in Germany, they are losing their origin in a physical way. One also has to understand and accept that the EU-market has many different regional and national characteristics, where 27 different problems cannot be solved by a single solution. Ideology should therefore not prevail, but realism and pragmatism, based on the common objectives and global legal settings. Perfect markets do not exist, not for electricity and not for gas either. Why not therefore be a little more realistic and interested in how to make it work, and if this is done in a dynamic sense, using benchmarking and best practice approaches. That would also allow regional markets to develop in specific ways in line with their specific characteristics and circumstances. Benchmarking and best practices could then give further ground for bridging regional differences on the basis of some further harmonization of rules and procedures, without running the risks of too many exemptions for specific national circumstances.

3.2.2 The CIEP-model

The ASCOS model (Ample, Secure, and Competitive Supplies) as developed by CIEP is illustrated by figure 9. It underlines the idea that the GTM should depart from the expected future developments in the gas market for the decades to come. Gas will be used, increasingly in power generation, but it has to compete with other fuels. Markets should offer a fair level playing field for this. On the supply side, as indicated in earlier sections, no matter what scenario is used, EU imports will have to increase and hence the EU should remain an attractive outlet for gas suppliers. This would be the more relevant as reductions in prices on the wholesale markets are primarily coming through competition in upstream markets and less on the downstream side. And finally, developments on both the demand and supply sides will lead to more cross border flows and thus more cross border investments.

Markets and regulation are the two sides of the same coin. Regulations are based on policy goals, which for energy are laid down in the TFEU, the Treaty on the Functioning of the EU. They are also the basis for the 3rd package, which gives some further specifications, such as the well-functioning of wholesale market in gas. This goal has to be added to the more important overlay to ensure ample supplies from outside the EU. In other words, the main goal should be the emergence of a well-functioning and transparent wholesale market with a high level of security of supply. Interestingly enough, the 3rd package gives no definition or further "critical success factors" for the functioning of wholesale markets. So, there is a need for interpretation, and hence discussion.

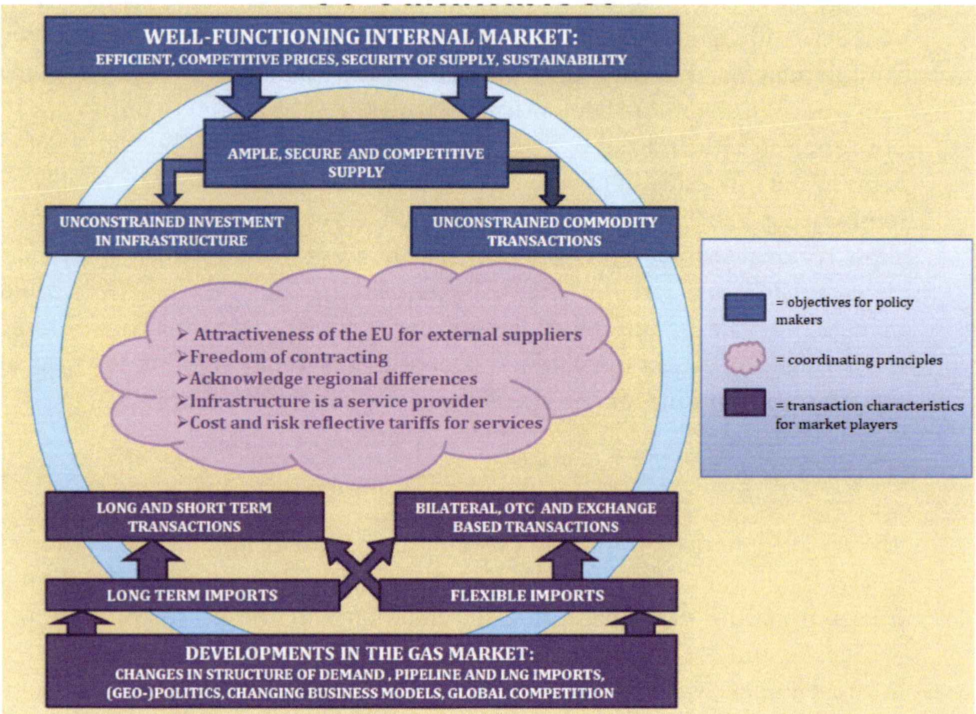

Figure 9. The ASCOS Model (CIEP)

The ASCOS-model departs therefore from the view that, both regarding the commodity side and transport side, market parties should be able to engage in commercial transaction meeting their needs. And on this basis, customized long term contracts will need to play a key role. It is important to note that no upstream project has ever been developed without a large part being committed under long term customized contracts. They would provide the best guarantee that gas supplies will come to the EU. Infrastructure is the other side of the coin, with customized long term capacity contracts. A key feature of markets is uncertainty. Market parties are in the best position to deal with this uncertainty and they will seek to develop mechanisms to manage these. Short term trade, be it on a spot basis or with additional timeframes are then coming up. It would be very imprudent for NRAs to formulate strict views or criteria for the relation between the various market structures. Markets cannot be designed by rules and regulations, but when market outcomes are not accepted in a broader or political sense, governments or NRAs may step in. Another point to take into account is the fact that within the EU and its markets, regional differences will have to be accepted, reflecting physical realities and structural conditions, including those in specific demand and supply structures. Regional markets therefore need to be seen as relevant and specific outcomes of market forces, and not always as "just" an intermediate stepping stone in the process towards a single EU market.

A smart balance is therefore needed between ex post and ex ante intervention in markets. Ex ante intervention is the rule for infrastructure and regulation. Ex post intervention is the rule for the market, and hence competition, competition policy and competition law. Being smart on the balance also means being smart on the "in-betweens". Examples on this last front are for instance coming from storage infrastructures and from LNG-terminals. Depending very much on the (regional) relevant market they are servicing, regulated or negotiated access has to be assessed. New investments in transmission are another example, when setting financial access conditions and assessing cost reflection and risk-reward balancing. Cross subsidization for instance between short- and long-haul transports should be limited and socialization be applied only in cases of a well-defined public need. This may then lead to customized contracts where tariff differentiation under non-discriminatory conditions is allowed.

3.2.3 Wholesale markets and their long-term and short-term characteristics

Wholesale markets are important components of any GTM-discussion. It goes without saying and it seems to be generally accepted that long term contracts made Europe more attractive for gas and are still extremely important for the security of demand and of supply and hence for the further development of the European gas market. Any GTM should therefore not give the impression to frustrate the existence of long-term contracts. Besides that, it is not for regulators to have an opinion on the kind of contracts market parties should sign and probably they have no competences to do that. Long term commodity contracts however do require some form of long term capacity contracts. Attention needs to be given to the role of the short term trading market. Short term trading, in the meaning of one to two years ahead, is a complementary feature to the longer term relations. Gas that is brought to the EU by a large number of long term contracts have usually price formulae in oil, but with various product specifications and time horizons. Therefore different contracts will have a different price at a different point in time at a different delivery point. What a traded market does is to find the optimum solution, a portfolio of optimization on a European scale, covering the use of long term contracts, of production wells, storages, regasification at terminals etc. as efficiently as possible in the interest of the end users. Discussion of traded markets in the GTM context is therefore by no means a move away from long term contracts.

These types of traded markets have developed in some EU countries at national or at regional levels. But other national markets that are using gas are still lacking this efficiency option, so it would be worthwhile to consider how and where to develop a complementary market. Slovenia could be seen as an example, but it would be unlikely to develop as a traded market with its small size, too little players and too small volumes. The question then is how to bring them into a price area with another neighboring market, maybe Austria or Italy, to foster the emergence of such a traded market. Could this be done by simply connecting Slovenia via efficient capacity allocation mechanisms to Austria and Italy, using the price signals from the gas hub Baumgarten? This may be unlikely, as a retail competitor on the Slovenian market can only compete on the basis of fixed price offers, for instance for a period of 12 months. In order to have a basis for its price quotation, the retail supplier has to look at the traded market and its price forward curve. And this requires a liquid forward market. The spot market cannot deliver such a quote as it is per definition much more volatile, sometimes even exaggerating price signals. Developing liquid forward markets is however more complicated than creating liquid spot markets. It needs many players to be active and much volume with many bids and offers.

If it works, the Slovenian retailer could take the price reference from Austria and now needs to ship the gas into Slovenia, covering its contract period starting for instance some months later. Under the current Baumgarten guidelines this would be the next frustration, as he has to wait for the next auction period for getting his capacity rights. This will bring him long on gas on Baumgarten and short on gas in Slovenia and in between no capacity. Such a situation does not foster retail competition. And this example could be one reason to get every end-user into a zone that is hosting a functioning forward market. This feature is a key component of the MECOS-model. The size of the zone is always a question but looking at physical realities, existing capacity between the Slovak Republic, Austria and the Czech Republic would do without any further investment to integrate Slovenia into that zone. It would also be easy to merge Spain and Portugal as well. It's a question of political will. In much the same vein, it could be mentioned that for instance in Munich a household or an end user can choose from some 80 or so fixed price offers with tenure of a year. All of this is based on forward market procurement. And although liquidity can always be better, the German NCG market is a prime example of the right direction when it comes to forward markets. Austria, however, has no liquid forward markets but a lot of voices from retail companies are saying that Austria should connect to NCG in order to have a forward market. It is a question for policy makers to take action. This merging approach, as suggested in the MECOS-Model, is different from market coupling, as it is no alternative. Market coupling can only couple spot markets as an effective means to manage congestion.

However, more is to be said about traded markets. Economic theory concludes that traded markets will depend on sufficient suppliers, perfect competitions means abundant supply. Connecting for instance Slovenia with Austria, Bulgaria, and even maybe Hungary into a well-functioning market does not bring per definition sufficient suppliers. All these markets are basically supplied one way or the other, by Gazprom. Extending market areas could indeed bring more liquidity, but a shortage, such as happened in the 2006 and 2009 Ukrainian crises, could lead to perverse price effects that would be detrimental for consumers. Therefore, one has to be very careful in designing of and focusing on traded markets. Another point of attention is that gas is a commodity, a commodity with specific quality versus location characteristics. There are many traded markets for goods in the world, i.e. metals, grain, apple juice, gas, etc. There is not a single market in the world with a liquid forward market. Forward markets, including the NBP market, are not liquid. There are many markets in these commodities and typically forward markets are more or less liquid for a period of maybe 2-3 months ahead and then it stops. The same would apply for other energy commodities, such as oil, coal and electricity. Market liquidity has a relatively short term focus, per definition. Supply functions may differ, but no energy commodity comes from a single source. Traders and market parties always have to make their own assessments about their risk-reward balance, depending on the various sources they can use or contract with. Liquidity as an objective for getting effective and efficient competition is therefore the wrong focus, but liquidity could be a useful indicator to assess competition.

3.2.4 Merging and/or connecting zones or markets

This issue is considered to be a key element in the GTM-discussion. Here again, words of warning are particularly voiced in relation to certain ex ante criteria to be fulfilled as a lead on to a prescriptive policy approach. Ex ante criteria such as a defined number of supply sources or the size of the market[9] could be useful as a starting point for reflection, but could also undermine market dynamics and contractual freedom. If such criteria are not met in a certain market zone, then connecting or merging with neighboring zones could become recommendable. If this is to be considered, it would be appropriate to make a sound analysis of the costs and the benefits. And this comes also to the issue on the optimal sizing of entry-exit zones. Market integration and trading crossing national borders will happen within and between entry/exit zones. The general idea is that the European market would be made up of several entry/exit zones. Some would even expect a single zone for the whole of the EU, but that is Utopian.

If the idea is to merge entry/exit zones into a single entry/exit structure, allowing gas to move anywhere freely within that merged zone without having to pay any more for transmission and to just nominate to exit it anywhere in that area, TSO- and national borders will be crossed without charges. In principle there's nothing wrong with that but it removes a source of funding. Transits crossing borders are very important in gas; in that sense it is not like electricity. Taking Belgium as an example, transits are probably two or three times as much as national consumption, requiring a lot of capacity. If these transits are not charged, then Belgian consumers are paying to fund the transit of gas that is consumed outside Belgium. Moving in that direction would need some kind of inter-TSO compensation mechanisms.

9 For instance, the MECOS-model (Glachant) mentions a minimal size of having 3 distinct supply sources and a market size of at least 20bcm/a for creating a well functioning wholesale market.

Such schemes may become relevant in future, but would bring quite some complicated regulatory challenges. TSOs would then be building capacity for the benefit of others and not charging those others. That does not seem to be a problem in principle, as an obvious approach to the European network would be to have some kind of TSO coordination at EU-level in order to decide what and where to build for the European market. In practice it could be very difficult. Coordination is difficult. ENTSO-G and ACER, the bodies that could be instrumental for such a mechanism, are still too young and have to prove their abilities. Other options are thinkable including devices where individual TSOs will decide and invest for transits and sell capacity rights to their neighboring TSOs who then could charge their markets. That would also require that TSOs need to take a view on the amount of capacity to be built in their neighboring market. It would be a recipe for confusion, potentially undermining security of supply. Connecting or merging market areas therefore needs very careful assessments.

Another important feature of this discussion is the role of hubs. Lessons from the US market are learning that there is room in the EU market for only a very limited number of really liquid hubs. Politicians, and sometimes regulators, seem to think that every national market would create the opportunity to have a hub. If that would be the way to go, only the interests of external suppliers are fostered, and not the interest of European consumers. Of course there may be several hubs. In the US there are plenty hubs, but most market liquidity is concentrated in a few hubs and the others are secondary, linked to the major hubs. They are bringing price differentials that are dependent on market situations, and sometimes also price alignments. So, there is no role for many liquid hubs in Europe, but one might expect developments that cross-border "hubbing" or moving gas from one entry/exit zone to another one is also the future of the EU gas market.

In order to achieve that, the European network code development should focus on a number of rather trivial, no regret improvements of technical harmonization. Operational balancing agreements, quality harmonization, standardization of some capacity products, standardization of business practices, such as the EasyGas process, they all could be effective and useful on the way towards further market integration. As a practical example, one could refer to Ireland and the UK. Ireland is an entry/exit zone, but not a liquid hub. They don't need a large connection capacity to the UK. If Irish market parties want to shop, they go virtually to the UK hub. There is no reason to develop one in Ireland. Such cases may also be relevant for other countries and areas as well. Market mergers and or zone mergers may be useful, but they must be analyzed on a case by case basis. Careful assessment of costs, transaction costs and capacity costs, are necessary. Costs will have to be traded against the benefits, especially the one from liquidity. They may not come if the objective market conditions are not fulfilled. That is a clear lesson from the American market.

3.2.5 Price alignment and liquidity

Here again, the GTM discussion tends to give quite some weight to these issues. Some are arguing that liquidity and price alignments have to be seen as objectives in order to develop (forward) traded market areas, by means of merging or some other connecting device. Others would argue that they could only be seen as relevant criteria for assessing for market developments[10]. Both parameters have basically a short term connotation and could definitely not match with the long term features of the market. For example assessing whether there is sufficient liquidity only makes sense when the assessment is based on the whole market (reflecting not only the exchanges, but also OTC-transaction and bilateral contracts). Precise definitions and statistical measuring are part of the difficulties that are faced in using liquidity as an indicator. Liquidity could be measured by different means, such as churn rates, or off-spreads. Statistical errors or even risks of manipulation could influence conclusions, but in a more general way, standardized criteria in a target-setting way could always inhibit market dynamics. Using liquidity to assess the success of EU gas markets is therefore not the way to go. If it would turn out that the case of a company, that started to buy via an exchange, chooses to conclude a long term bilateral contract, would be perceived as a reduction in liquidity. This would be regarded as a setback, while it enhances supply security.

Price alignment is used by some as an argument to connect markets, as price differentials are by definition seen as a result of too little competition. Price differentials between two neighboring markets do not always reflect the risk of some form of market abuse, but could usually be explained by a number of aspects, such as differences in market structures and institutions, fuel mix policies, unforeseen demand due to changing weather conditions, taxation

10 See for instance Glachant's paper on the MECOS-model, pages 8-9.

and alike. It could also be considered as a relevant market signal to the need for investing in infrastructures such as pipelines and storage capacity. A single gas price in the EU for instance would imply that any new LNG terminal in the EU should be built in Greece. There is no need to strive for price alignment. If prices in the Netherlands and UK are the same it could well mean that the UK needs storage. And if they do not deviate there will not be any storage built in the UK, probably slightly more expensive than in the northern part of Germany. Statistics are also a difficulty, such as with liquidity, to be overcome when prices are compared. Here again, it would be a risk if price aligning becomes a political need, but price assessments and understanding differentials could be very useful in relation to market developments and market behaviors.

3.2.6 Cross-Border capacity, congestion, allocation and markets

Whatever model or approach is chosen about further connecting market areas, the issue of long-term capacity allocation seems to be unavoidable. There is a market for commodity, but there clearly is a growing need to consider effective European capacity-markets as well. A market that would be instrumental in allocating long-term capacity rights, subject to tight congestion management provisions. Without these any long term allocation would be risky and tends to restrict existing capacities to reserved rights from earlier decades. The more effective (contractual) congestion management, the more capacity allocation on a long term basis would be possible. One way of approaching this issue is via a process of advanced and modified open seasons, integrating and coordinating across several entry/exit zones and across national borders. Participation in the process should not be limited to supply companies, to shippers, but governments, regulators, and other TSOs should be playing a role as well. Such a process could also give due account to the need for longer term capacity rights.

Enhancing effective interconnections for the European market cannot be reached without the role of long term capacity contracts. It is a question that the whole gas industry will have to face and open seasons to date did not always give the right opportunities to invest in new capacity. In specific cases public money from the EU was required and that may even be the case for the future. But one should be very careful in using that option. If the market sees no reason to invest, it could either be that the regulatory framework does not provide the right condition, or there simply is no real market need. The proposed EU Regulation on Energy Infrastructures [11] presents an opportunity for the NRAs and ACER to adapt regulatory approaches to meet the interests of new cross-border investments. In case there is no alternative for financing specific new transmission capacity, EU public funds could be considered as really a last resort, under stringent and carefully framed conditions and criteria. This could be a solution for certain areas but not for the current European network and especially not in the northwestern part.

Anyway, the coordinated approaches suggested would also be good for supply security, but this is not the only aspect. Competition in capacity might also be worthwhile pursuing, as scarcity in transmission capacity is not to stay per definition. One main lesson from the American model is that regulation and competition can go hand in hand. Regulation of transmission or transportation may also be necessary, but competition can take place even under regulation. Some kind of harmonized regulation would then be required, especially for the cross-border context. Although for tariff regulation EU regulators tend to follow similar approaches, but some monitoring exercise would be very useful. Regulation 715 gives already some provisions that clearly indicate that monitoring of tariff setting criteria, including tariff structures, could be done.

Assessing future needs in relation to managing cross border capacity developments and the role of open seasons, it would be useful to reflect also on the structural developments that are taking place in and for the TSOs themselves. The 3rd package clearly gives regulatory options for further strengthening their independence, meaning that already as of March 2012 they need to be really independent. Regardless of which model they choose, it will have an effect on the way they are being regulated. They shouldn't be regulated as though they are still part of this integrated company with all the links with production, trade and supply that could result from that. That will and should have an effect on how regulation works, even for the internal networks. This is something to take account of.

All these ideas for more cross-border coordination would further the development of cross-border markets, allowing hubs to be emerging when market conditions are right. ACER could be key in this respect, focusing its mandate for enhancing inter-NRA cooperation to bring them together

11 Proposed Regulation on "Guidelines for trans-European energy infrastructure"...
See http://eur-lex.europa.eu/LexUriServ/LexUriServ.do?uri=CELEX:52011PC0658:EN:NOT

and set them to work. To work on making trans-border open seasons a functioning process, which is presently not the case with the recent examples for the interconnection between Slovakia and Hungary and the one between Germany and Poland? These two procedures were fully unmatched, no common allocation rules, no common commercialization of products and no common time origin. To work also on the monitoring of tariff structures and settings, exploring the right regulatory conditions for matching risk-reward balancing in new investments and for developing sound tools for analyzing cross-border cost/benefits.

3.2.7 Regional differences and regional markets

There is a risk that the GTM-discussion would become too theoretical, not considering the actual functioning of gas markets in the EU, where major regional differences do exist. It is sometimes heard that one-fits-all approaches should the way forward. Especially when too much attention is paid to specific problems in specific regions and or markets. Such one -fits-all approach might be counterproductive. For instance if it might for sound reasons be useful to introduce market-coupling in a certain area and to go for a pilot in exploring the potentials, this would not mean to say that for other areas similar solutions should be considered. Or, when a particular market environment might be trying to discourage the role of long-term contracts and is able to strongly emphasize spot markets due to its particular supply situation, this would also not be the obvious way forward for continental markets with different supply possibilities.

These sometimes detailed proposals and approaches are also seen in the context of the ongoing discussions on the framework guidelines and network codes for capacity management and congestion management. To translate these specifics into a GTM would again create severe difficulties as -in a more general way- a GTM is just supposed to be global and forward looking by nature, with sufficient room for market circumstances and conditions in different parts of the EU. It would therefore be necessary to take duly account of what really is happening in specific regional markets and us e that as a basis to work on in the particular market areas. The GTM should try to accommodate these developments in a coherent way.

On the other hand, it goes without saying that the present process for implementing the 3rd package is moving and going. A GTM should give the relevant focus, and could anyway result in a vision that is really in line with developments in NW-European markets and a second vision that gives the right framing for the markets in the Southeast. The MECOS-model as proposed also has these kind of alternatives in it with the market-area and trading region model. The trading region model could maybe more interesting for some countries in central and eastern EU markets, whereas merging of market areas might be the way to go for western areas. The ASCOS-model also stresses the point of regional differences. The big question however for moving towards a single market remains on the table, i.e. how to bridge these differences. Harmonization might be a key word to that, an easy word for a very difficult process. If this is not happening, many requests for exemptions to the codes and the guidelines may be expected, simply since the regions, the regulators and the TSOs are not ready for moving towards more harmonization, for instance on balancing or on coordinated open seasons as earlier mentioned.

The same would apply to tariff differentials for transmission. On the basis of the non-discrimination principle such differentials, that might be a sound conclusion as a result of open seasons for new builds and customized long-term contract, should be looked at with skepticism and reluctance. Especially when this is accepted in an up-front process. It may well be in an auction process that is designed to look some 10-15 years ahead, even when quarterly products for 15 years are for sale, long term bookings in terms of a capacity price might be relevant. But to start upfront by introducing tariff differentials for long term bookings may not be the right one. And here again, differentials and differences in market conditions might be sound outcomes, accepting regional approaches and regional differences.

3.2.8 The external supplier perspective

More different views on the GTM-discussion are coming from the perspective context of the EU's external suppliers and the more particular microeconomic realities. If different suppliers are competing with each other bringing gas from the same supply source, one could argue whether that is a real market. It is not the market where gas supplies are competing for market shares, having price competition. The upstream supply side is based on a handful of suppliers. It is therefore an oligopoly. The question is how to face an oligopoly. This cannot be done by regulation. The EU cannot dream anymore of regulating Russia, Algeria, Norway and the others as was done in the old days, some 10-15 years ago. All major national countries had their single buyers, finding out that it was better to cooperate than to compete. On the upstream side suppliers have learned that lesson. In the EU's Northern Dimension Norway and Russia in reality don't try to undercut each other. Would LNG change the game? We see in today's world that Russia and Qatar seem to divide the market, where Qatar will continue to focus on Asia as these consumers are still happy with some form of oil price related conditions, leaving the price destructions from spot markets to the Russians to face.

On the other hand, these suppliers are facing the new unbundled world of natural monopolies in transmission. Hence the major companies coming from the outside are facing a variety of buyers and re-sellers and some oligopolistic devices in transmission. Regulated entities however with different national regulatory authorities, not a single one. And also a rather vague discussion on competition, on liberalization and on privatization. Is there an EU answer on facing oligopolies that supply crucial amounts of gas to the EU market? And what is the view on the variety of monopolistic TSOs with an increasingly common network crossing national borders that are regulated by different national entities? Where in the GTM is there a vision on this, or at least some kind of recognition? Questions that are maybe too tough to answer now, but in the post 2020 context they should be a relevant part of any EU gas security of supply architecture.

3.2.9 The way forward for GTM?

The process of setting a number of specific framework guidelines as a basis for the Network Codes is continuing. Continuing with many consultations with stakeholders, with sometimes intense discussions and sometimes not. The whole thing is under some political pressure by the February 2011 Council conclusion to finalize the internal energy market by 2014/15. Being specific on sometimes very detailed issues is running the risk of missing the overall perspective. And there the Gas Target Model has to come in.

The various workshop discussions that took place in 2011 were clearly indicating that there are still a number of very relevant issues in a GTM that are not yet fully digested, understood, or let only concluded in a coherent and consistent way. Locking people up for a week or so to let it happen would sound nice, but is not realistic. One has to realize that in an ideal world a GTM was formulated before or maybe during the negotiations of the 3rd package[12]. That was not possible either. One has to realize that the process is one that is still coming from 27 member states, with different markets and history, with different stakeholders and sometimes very deeply founded strategic security considerations. We have to recognize that it is a process to ensure that the framework guidelines and guidelines are not contradicting and are really interlinking with each other. This is a major task for both the NRA's and ACER, together with ENTSO-G.

It looks as if these concerns were reflected in the CEER vision for the Gas target model that was published in December 2011[13]. This vision uses the three main pillars that seem to be widely accepted, i.e. "enabling functioning wholesale markets", "connecting functioning wholesale markets" and "ensuring secure supply and economic investment". Each of these pillars then results in some specific recommendations for NRAs and stakeholders to consider in the decision-making process on the Network Codes. It also reflects the dynamic nature of the GTM, to be further evaluated and assessed in the coming years.

The thinking about the GTM should therefore continue. In a way, it may even be uncoupled from the process of implementing the 3rd package. Gas is to stay in the foreseeable EU energy mix. Its role will change, especially in power generation with its characteristics of being a very flexible fuel to manage the growing role of intermittent energy sources. This role will bring challenges that go beyond the 3rd package, both in terms of business models with suppliers and on using infrastructures. New market and regulatory designs might be needed to meet these challenges. But, realism should prevail. ACER, regulators or policy makers should not interpret their roles as "knowing better than the market" and market parties should understand and consider how to act in a balance between ex post and *ex ante* interventions by the respective market and regulatory authorities. That would include the need to find a way in creating joint understandings between oligopolistic supply structures and non-oligopolistic demand structures in a context of semi-monopolistic vital infrastructures.

12 It would be interesting to note that a draft GTM, as a so called "strategy paper", was already formulated in the beginning of the Madrid Process and was considered as a useful vision to continue to work on. The paper is still available at the EU Energy website under the 4th meeting of the Florence Forum and is giving also today some food for thought.

13 See CEER Conclusions Paper on the GTM, Ref: C11-GWG-82-03 on the CEER website.

There may however still be some quick wins to consider, where especially ACER could move on the basis of the Gas Regulation. A process of coordinated and timely auctions for short-term capacity allocations at borders, maybe together with some interoperability measures. If these and some other basic congestion management procedures were in place, "the Slovenia trader" would probably be in a better position. This shouldn't be too difficult to start with. Also the region in Southeastern Europe and their developments towards proper functioning markets have substantial infrastructure that is not used as it is even still far from any 2nd package requirements. It is for instance impossible to understand why Bulgaria remained without gas in 2009 when it is connected by two pipelines to LNG terminals in the region that could physically provide more than twice the Bulgarian demand. Such issues and maybe some more could be seen as negotiable points in a win-win situation between the EU and Gazprom in the South Stream dossier. A further quick win might be found in the harmonization process of a number relatively easy and detailed but important elements with respect to cross-border trade, including ones on coordination procedures for auctions, tariff harmonization devices and the "gas day" definition. All these quick wins might be further considered before any more far-reaching approaches are introduced.

CHAPTER III

THE BUILDING OF ENERGY SOLIDARITY IN THE EU

Nicole Ahner, European University Institute
Jean-Michel Glachant, European University Institute

1. Introduction

Back in 1973, the Netherlands was confronted with the Arab Oil Embargo. The Dutch government sought solidarity in Brussels. It did not get it. It was impossible to come to a solidarity scheme sharing available oil supplies. The Netherlands was on its own. The fact that France and the UK continued to receive oil supplies made it even more difficult to come to grips with achieving solidarity, even for the European Commission. It was then that a US proposal for an emergency oil allocation scheme led to 'solidarity', eventually materializing as the International Energy Agency (IEA).

This chapter is not about the oil crisis. It is about solidarity. Solidarity lies at the heart of any gas security of supply architecture.

While situations like the oil embargo do not occur every day, they do – albeit in different shapes – occur: the January 2009 gas crisis, where the transit of Russian gas to Europe through the Ukraine was interrupted, being just one example. Yet, the curious thing in this context is the question of 'why solidarity is needed in these cases?' Intuitively, one should assume that it is the Internal Energy Market that provides market situations that, first of all, prevent supply crisis, and, in case an emergency arises, nonetheless deliver those remedies best able to cope with such emergency. In other words, is 'solidarity' actually needed where different market situations are already addressed by internal market-based relationships? This question is inextricably linked with the question of what the Internal Energy Market delivers and what it does not. Considering the guarantor role of the internal market for security of supply: is solidarity then an empty formula or a negligible appendix to market-based instruments? How is solidarity translated into actions? Or, in other words, which tools are at hand at EU level to translate solidarity into concrete actions? Building on the relevant experiences made by the Member States during the EU's January 2009 gas supply crisis and factoring in the gas industry's, the regulator's, the European Commission's, as well as energy doctrine's approach to solidarity, this chapter tries to shed some light on these questions. The fact that the January 2009 gas crisis has been the most serious supply crisis in Europe – the share of lost gas supply in the countries in the affected region from Austria to Greece amounted to 50-100 percent – makes this case so interesting for the purpose of our discussion. It qualifies as an unprecedented supply security experiment that tested the EU's vulnerability to natural gas supply security risks.

2. The concept of solidarity in the EU energy policy context

Solidarity is an old-fashioned concept that dates back at least 30 years. It is currently in the process of being restyled. The Lisbon Treaty gave new impetus to solidarity's role in energy policy, by leading *inter alia* to inclusion of solidarity within the Treaty of the Functioning of the European Union (TFEU). Article 194, paragraph 1 of the TFEU calls for the pursuit of EU energy policy objectives *in a spirit of solidarity between Member States.*

The most recent manifestation of this development towards an enshrinement of solidarity is found in EU secondary legislation, namely the new 2010 Gas Security of Supply Regulation (Regulation (EU) No 994/2010). This new energy security tool is supposed to manage unforeseen gas supply interruptions. It deals with crisis management on a short-term basis, defining a common minimum level of risk that should be applied among the European countries. *Pre*-crisis – it tackles solidarity in the sense that it prepares the Member States for emergencies requiring unique EU-wide standards imposed on all Member States for preparatory reasons; at times of emergencies it intervenes to ensure solidarity. Mutual support between the Member States is guaranteed by both EU level coordination and regional cooperation. Regulation (EU) No 994/2010 is a good foundation on which solidarity can be built.

Now, let us attempt to define what 'solidarity' actually means in the specific context at issue. With regard to gas security of supply, it can be said that solidarity consists of three interacting pillars "rules, behaviors and assets respectively aiming at enhancing supply security."

In theory, solidarity between two or more Member States for their gas supply simply means that 'one Member State helps the other one when it needs it.' In practice, it is more difficult because there is the legal and regulatory framework in place in each country, as well as at the European level, which set the rules. Then there are a host of actors in the gas sector: the Transmission System Operators (TSOs), the shippers and the end users, each following its own set of rules.

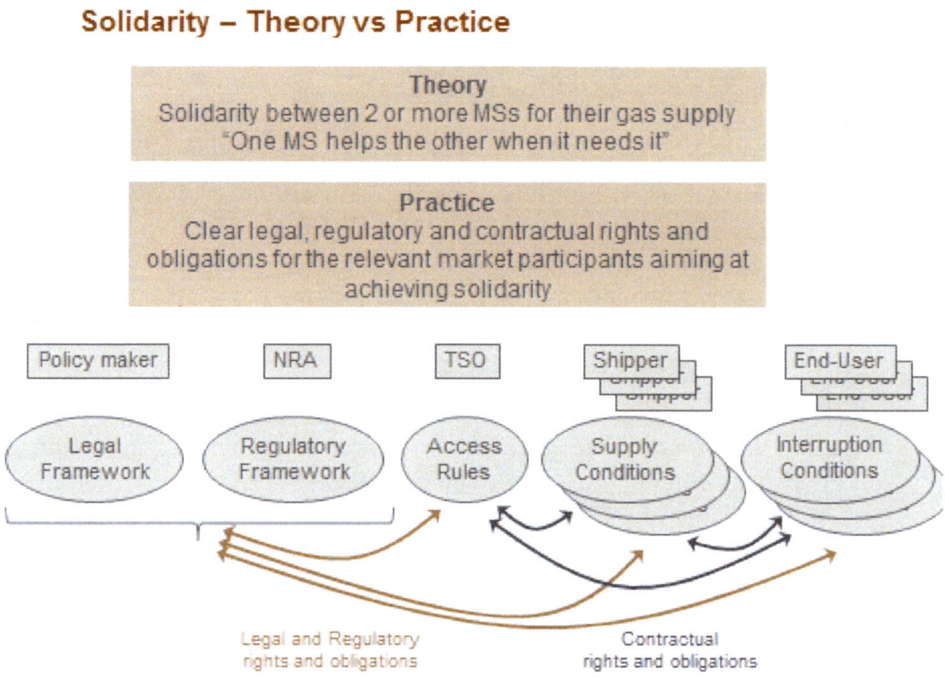

Source: Fluxys 2011

Together, these considerations create a general scheme for each Member State. Member States can then ensure additional solidarity mechanisms through their own national legal and regulatory frameworks. Despite this heterogeneous web of supranational rules, national rules and the various actors involved, solidarity must work in practice. Although this is difficult, there is some progress visible. One example is the EU-wide standards introduced by the Regulation (EU) No 994/2010 already mentioned above. However, the legal and regulatory framework is not currently complete. Regulation (EU) No 994/2010 must still be implemented for the large part, especially the preventative action plans. Once all of these pieces are put in place, parties will have clearer roles and responsibilities, including contractual obligations. If these frameworks are in place, they can provide for the solidarity, in which market participants, TSOs and end-users will all participate. In fact, market participants are neutral with regard to the security of supply objective. If security of supply is foreseen as a goal, i.e. the market participants are given constraints or they are incentivized respectively, they will do what they are required to do in order to reach it. However, if they are not obliged to do so, they will not. This means that once the right framework managing the rules is set and fully implemented, market participants will act accordingly and should all go in the right direction.

Anyway, full implementation of such rules is certainly not the end of ambiguities. As briefly mentioned above, there are at least four key players involved in solidarity decisions. They are the TSOs, the regulatory authorities, the shippers, the Member State governments and a kind of 'European government', that is the European Commission. What remains unclear is who is leading and who is doing what *ex ante*, and, in particular, *on the spot*. *Ex ante*, there is the risk assessment, the preventative action plan, the emergency plans which have to be done. There are the Member States, the Commission, and the competition authorities in each State, who make all the plans. But they have to decide who will work in case of a crisis 'on the spot', who is responsible for what and how it will happen. The procedures will have to be defined by these people. In addition, it has to be taken into account that the responsible actor may also appoint others. As a consequence, the number of actors whose responsibilities need to be defined and coordinated increases additionally.

Moreover, a crisis happens unexpectedly and unpredictably. It will not always be possible to treat a crisis as it is imagined in the emergency plan. The emergency plan should anticipate the mechanisms that will be activated when a crisis should arise. However, it will not be possible that the emergency plans will precisely define 'when A happens, you have to do X, Y and Z'. Moreover, even with the right framework in place stating which measure will be applied at which moment, there will always be the unavoidable and not predictable interim step of defining how to precisely follow the plans on the spot, i.e. when the crisis actually happens.

2.1 Solidarity – *ex ante* and on the spot

Naturally, solidarity is required not only during crisis periods but also before a crisis arises. Yet, our core assumption is the already-mentioned differentiation between *ex ante* solidarity, i.e. solidarity that takes place before the crisis occurs (making 95 percent of the solidarity) and *on the spot* solidarity i.e. solidarity that takes place during a supply crisis (making 5 percent of it). It may be said that solidarity in the sense of preventing supply crisis is exercised in a more rational way, while solidarity action during the emergency case – due to the values at stake and the heterogeneity of national interests – happens in a less clear way.

Ex ante, in order to prevent supply crisis, institution building such as the building of the internal gas market is key to accumulate assets to prevent an emergency case. In fact, institution building has proven to be an appropriate way to express solidarity *ex ante*. The European tool of choice for securing gas supply is still a well-functioning internal gas market. Looking at the January 2009 crisis the market proved to be able to deliver market based solutions for most of crisis' duration, with the exception of a few regions in Eastern Europe. Conversely, in Western Europe, very big changes in flow were possible to be achieved very quickly under market conditions. However, to make such an approach fully effective, a well-functioning market (i.e. liquid and attractive for both suppliers and consumers) that is connected to available capacity and sufficiently flexible to weather any supply shortage, must be reached. This is not yet the case in the EU.

In this context, an important question is also whether a distinction should be made between when the market is considered working and when an emergency starts. Very simply, an emergency starts when the market is not working anymore. If, at the time an incident occurs, the market is functioning well, the market will provide the solution. Of course, there will be a delay in providing this solution since the market cannot always react in only one hour. If the market, for instance, needs to activate production or storage, or gas needs to arrive from other countries, then – assuming the need for big quantities – it will take approximately 4-6 hours, which is not a lot of time. But, there is the need for something in the interim. An appropriate tool to address this interim period of time could be an action by the TSO before the market is able to fully react. What has been seen, for instance, in the Ukrainian crisis is that it took roughly one or two days to have the full reverse flows and capacity up to 25 bcm. So, a full market reaction may take some time; therefore the TSO should act in the interim. TSO action in this case is a non-market based tool to be exercised before a market based reaction is able to achieve its full effect, i.e. if the market reaction at one point appears to be insufficient, it is time to start non-market-based measures. The portion of Regulation (EU) No 994/2010 dealing with this issue is not very clear. If at this point some clarity would be provided, sudden crises could probably be managed. As an example: if a State declares an emergency there is the possibility that the Commission requests modifications. Being notified, either about the subsequent modification or of the reasons for disagreement with the Commission's request for modifications, the Commission gets three days to either amend or withdraw its request (Article 10 (8)). Such cumbersome procedural steps might be difficult for Member States to follow in emergency situations. If there is a crisis the Member State might declare an emergency and take measures but it will not come back three days later. Another issue is the escalation procedure foreseen on the regional scale, on the European scale and where solidarity comes in. Member States will have to cut demand. It is necessary that a mechanism is put in place to know 'who has to be cut'. Here governments will have a critical role to play: what level is a country ready to give to another country? This may be a purely political decision at this point in time.

Obviously, it must not be ignored that preparing for an emergency case as a group is also about getting to a solution that maximizes the welfare of the group as opposed to the welfare of the individual State. Here the typical problems discussed in the economic literature concerning collective action[14] come to the fore. It is indeed very difficult to create a joint solution and find solutions that maximize joint welfare because very sophisticated site payment schemes and guarantees need to be in place.

On the spot, i.e. with regard to the emergency case, the big questions are related to how to ensure that during the emergency the different group members, the Member States, will show a commitment to respect those contracts that were concluded before the emergency case and will allow the market to function even during an emergency. Contractual arrangements should ensure

14 Such as for instance Olson.M (1965) The Logic of Collective Action, Harvard University Press, Cambridge: Massachusetts; Ostrom.E (1990) Governing the
Commons: The Evolution of Institutions for Collective Action, Cambridge University Press: New York.

that efficient and sufficient capacity is in place to meet the demand at all times. These contractual arrangements may serve two purposes. The first is to underpin any required investment by booking the necessary capacity. The second is to ensure that the gas will actually flow when it is needed. Regional risk assessments could actually be used to assess where and whether such backup arrangements may be necessary. But of course it is up to the Member States themselves to effectuate those or not. This is in line with the Regulation (EU) No 994/2010.

The first reaction in emergencies is usually that the national bodies concentrate on the local welfare and try to ensure a supply most of all for their citizens and not for the neighbours and/or the others of the group. It can be said that if a well-functioning market is missing, solidarity might be a substitute for markets to serve consumers. Of course, in these times part of the welfare has to be given up to help others so that no price advantage is exploited in this act.

2.2 Actors and contributions

The market will deliver the best mechanism for supporting security of supply and to act in a crisis. What is the role then of solidarity and how can the EU, the NRAs and the Member States demonstrate solidarity?

2.2.1 European Union

The role of the EU (i.e., the Commission) consists in proposing a "good" that is an appropriate legal framework. Risk to a good framework is incoherence. What is a "good" proposal? To answer the question with a question: Are exemptions and financial incentives really wise? The possibility of an exemption may remove the incentive to make an investment without exemptions. Are the additional financial incentives as foreseen in the recent energy infrastructure package necessary? Of course, such incentives might be good for some projects that would not be built without these financial incentives. However, now of course it must be assumed that every TSO investor will try to get into that legal framework in order to maybe get something more.

One of the utmost important things on the Commission side is to watch the timely implementation of the *acquis* in order to speak the same language in all Member States. There are still a couple of countries that have not yet transposed the Second Package. Persisting differences in transposition lead to countries being at different levels. The key problem with the actual enforcement of new legislation is the lengthiness involved in possible infringement procedures for enforcing implementation. Moreover, whenever there are problems the Commission very quickly reacts and proposes new pieces of legislation.

Another area of increased EU involvement is the foreign energy relations area. The Commission, since 2010, has started to intervene more and more in this field, which has always been dominated by bilateral energy deals between Member States and the major supplier countries. In fact, even today, this area of energy policy is considered a national issue. The situation is aggravated by the fact that transparency in this area is lacking almost completely. The Member States, following a go-it-alone attitude, conclude bilateral deals with major energy suppliers without coordinating with, either, the Commission or the other Member States. Particularly from the third country perspective such practice puts into question the cohesiveness and the credibility of the EU energy external policy. Conservative estimates suggest that at the time being around 90 oil and gas intergovernmental agreements exist between Member States and third countries. This prevailing practice has proven to present some serious drawbacks for the EU as a whole. It has not only prevented the ability of the EU to "speak with a single voice," a grievance that above all weakened the negotiating position of the Union versus key producer countries (e.g., Russia, which may use the intransparency to enhance its prize negotiation position). Where politicians were involved in the negotiation process, inconsistency derived also from changes of these responsible politicians due to, for instance, the end of their mandate: making it possible that different individuals participate as energy ministers in a single negotiation. Obviously, such practice was not a good signal to the EU's negotiating partners. The 2011 Energy Council then concluded *inter alia* that *'There is a need for better coordination of EU and Member States' activities with a view to ensuring consistency and coherence in the EU's external relations with key producer, transit, and consumer countries.'* Finally, on 7th September 2011 the European Commission issued its long anticipated Communication on security of energy supply and international cooperation proposing concrete instruments on how energy foreign relations should be addressed in the future. In sum, the current action of the EC walks the line between the respect for the Member States sovereignty in exercising their foreign relation policies and the need to ensure their compliance with the EU legal order. It can be said that convergence is about to take place between the EU and its Member States leading to a common foreign energy policy.

The role of the EU (Commission)
• Propose the appropriate European legal framework • Watch and enforce its implementation • Take a strong role with regards to external energy relations

2.2.2 Member States

How can Member States demonstrate solidarity? *Ex ante.* First of all, the Member States task demonstrating solidarity is the full and rapid transposition of the EU energy *acquis.* A stable regulatory framework needs to be created in order that investors can trust in the market, as well as in the responsible institutions such as the governments and authorities involved. To date, for instance, it is difficult to attract private investment in energy infrastructure in southeast Europe. Practicing solidarity in these areas also means enabling such solidarity by investing that which is required for a necessary, secure regulatory and legal framework.

Next, a clear definition of roles and responsibilities is needed at the national level. *Ex ante*, before the crisis takes place, the government has to assign the right bodies, their responsibilities and tasks: What is the regulator doing? What is the TSO and the Independent System Operator (ISO) doing? What are the market participants doing? What shall happen when it comes to real supply crisis measures, who to disconnect first and which effect does this have on the overall economy? If the big consumers, such as power stations, are disconnected first this would also cause an electricity crisis. Therefore, there needs to be clear planning so that the involved parties know what to do when a crisis takes place. It is not the ministers and the governments who solve those issues at the very last minute and can provide the right answers to these questions.

One lesson learned from the January 2009 crisis was that the biggest problems arised in those countries where these preparations were not made. Nobody knew what to do. Of course, the preparation of an adequate emergency planning takes time. One country that may serve as a good example may be Austria. After it had in 2006 a crisis it started out emergency planning and continuously tests it.

Areas of improvement – What needs to be done at Member State level in terms of improvement? A regional mechanism for TSOs is needed for the optimization of gas flows. Another key issue is transparency. Transparency is of utmost importance because information flows are indispensable in a crisis. The emergency plans need to be coordinated to avoid unilateral measures at the expense of other Member States. Against such a background, active participation in regional and EU bodies for coordination and info exchange is essential part of demonstrating solidarity.

How can Member States demonstrate solidarity?
• Full and rapid transposition of the EU energy acquis • Creating a stable national regulatory framework to ensure trust in the market, government/authorities • Clear definition of roles and responsibilities of actors • Ensure transparency, enhance information flow • Active participation in regional and EU bodies (coordination and info exchange)

2.2.3 National Regulatory Authorities

From a regulator's perspective, there are two main tools for contributing to solidarity. First, there are the tariffs by which investments are recovered. It is, thus, about how to create the right investment framework for new investments to be realized. Second, is the setting of market rules. Framework guidelines for tariffication that define how to design the new tariff for the future European gas market are currently being drafted within the Agency for the Cooperation of Energy Regulators (ACER). There are some upfront challenges in that the 3rd Energy Package requires that each Member State has an entry/exit system for the tariff. But, at the same time, while designing a well-functioning internal gas market, there might be a risk of pancaking as the tariffs cannot be cost reflective, and, as a consequence, can create market distortions. The gas is not flowing in the right direction because of some tariff constraints. Thus the question is whether it is the best approach to have one entry exit system for each Member State or if broader entry/exit areas encompassing more than one single system should be envisaged. However, creating and broadening this entry/exit system would mean that some interconnection points would no longer be booked. Thus one arrives at the point of needing to identify an inter-TSO compensation scheme. In the case of electricity, it was a difficult task to get such a compensation scheme. In the case of gas, it may be easier. For electricity, the main problem is that the causality of flows can hardly be determined. Conversely, for gas, this should not be a problem. It should be rather easy to identify the flows and thus to split the respective costs among the interested TSOs.

How do NRAs contribute to solidarity?
• Tariff setting to create the right investment framework • Setting of market rules

2.2.4 Transmission System Operators

At the time of the crisis, not all regions of Europe were provided with gas. Against such a background, even the TSOs have been blamed for not taking the necessary actions. When attempting to identify culprits, the fact that these actors were asked to perform operations that they have never been asked to perform previously needs to be taken into account. It was only after the crisis that there were new requirements to bring gas from the West to the East. A lot of TSOs have tried very ingenious solutions and the whole industry has tried to manage the crisis doing as much as possible. TSOs managed to maximize flows, storage was offered above the maximum capacity of the storage installations, liquefied natural gas (LNG) receiving terminals were used extensively and cargo was diverted to the places where it was needed. In sum, it can be said that it was the industry that accomplished a big part of the job. For the infrastructure operators, it is easier to determine who did what. The contribution of the shippers and commodity part was, of course, key to bring gas to the places where it was needed. Infrastructure operators have experience of cooperation (such as in exchanging data for planning infrastructure for daily discussions between dispatching of flows, etc.). Solidarity and exchange of information is something that has existed since gas started crossing borders. In fact, 'information flow' was key during the January 2009 gas crisis, not only to enable the European Commission to fulfill its coordination and supporting role, but also for the overall management of the crisis. It was the first time that a European crisis had the consequence that communication only with the neighboring TSOs was not enough. In the case of a European crisis, the European coordination that was needed already had been taken over by the European Commission. The problem was that the exchange of information and the overall communication was not formalized.

However, this situation has been improved since then. The information that the European Commission needed during the crisis is now available. On top of that, storage and LNG operators are developing common templates which will make it easier for storage users and terminal users to find the right information in the right place.

The question of how TSOs should nominate storage arose at the moment the crisis occurred. Should the private contracts be respected and the nomination of private players accepted in a situation when the whole network flow system was in a critical state? How to keep the system balanced when some private players would like to nominate storage, i.e. when gas storage that would be needed for system balancing is needed somewhere else? TSOs do and should play a key role in crisis management. Therefore it is very important to define *ex ante* what special rights the TSO might have under these special conditions. For example in Hungary the government, until the end of the crisis, did not officially announce that it was a crisis situation because, if it would have done so, the TSO would have had the right to these special nominations and a lot of private contracts would have been hurt. Naturally, the government had to fear potential post-crisis litigation procedures from private players. For this reason, the TSO had to re-nominate dozens of times within the day, always calling its partners. It was a kind of 'management on the spot'. It will be much more comfortable for the TSOs in this situation to be able to base its operations and decisions on clear rules that are set up *ex ante*, defining precisely what the TSO can and cannot do. It is then up to the Commission and governments in regional cooperation to set up institutions that allow all players to discuss what to do in the event of a crisis.

Note that following several critiques against TSOs for not having provided the right solutions and infrastructure, Gas Infrastructure Europe (GIE) started a study right after the 2009 crisis on reverse flows. The study started from the situation during the crisis and later extended to the EU. It looked at where the bottlenecks were and notified all of the TSOs where small projects could lead to improvements. This was done in coordination with the European Commission. Most of these projects are already implemented. The Recovery Programme gave the necessary push to realize these projects. 45 projects had been identified at the time that the GIE report was published in 2009. It can be considered being a kind of pre-study in the kind of preventative action plan that is now foreseen in the Regulation (EU) No 994/2010. It is a brainstorming of what can be done effectively.

How do TSOs contribute to solidarity?
• Crisis management 'on the spot' • Inter-TSO information exchange

2.3 Infrastructure investment as basis for solidarity

While infrastructure at the time of the crisis played a very important role in terms of providing solutions, it is, nevertheless, also considered as the source of the problem. A prerequisite to allowing the building of the required infrastructure is a sound investment climate. While this sounds simple and logical, such a climate does not yet exist. In order to create this investment climate for new infrastructure, it was necessary to set up National Regulatory Authorities (NRAs) in each Member State and ACER. Moreover, the European Network of Transmission System Operators for Gas (ENTSO-G) has been developing, as part of its legal tasks, a number of instruments to help assess where these investments will be needed. Among these instruments is the 10 Year Network Development Plan and the summer and winter outlooks (all published on the ENTSO-G website). In addition ENTSO-G has been performing specific studies such as a study on reverse flow – about where and what kind of reverse flow is needed. That would cover most situations, but of course it still leaves open what would happen if a particular situation arises that has not been foreseen and for which backup arrangements are not yet in place.

In the past the gas industry, at least in some parts of Europe, did not make the necessary investment to provide the required infrastructure. For example, looking at central Eastern Europe, it has had for the last 20 years the same infrastructure that it inherited from the past. Nothing much happened since political changes. This is a complete different situation as compared to the situation in electricity. In electricity, the full reorientation of the central Eastern European electricity system into the Union for the Co-ordination of Transmission of Electricity (UCTE) took place. A huge number of new lines have been put in place and full re-integration of the electricity grid of that region into UCTE took place. Such reorientation and/or change is fully missing in the gas sector. The non-cooperating lines are prevailing in most parts of that region.

Public intervention One option for tackling the problem of strategic underinvestment at government level is the provision of public money. An example of such an approach is the strategic storage site in Hungary. It came to life because the government aimed at an improvement of storage and interconnectivity which the national incumbent was not delivering at that time. In the end, politicians decided to change the situation by putting public money into it, thus somehow handling the problem of strategic underinvestment in gas infrastructure. It appears that part of the reaction from the European Commission today to put public money into the system and to bring a political solution to this issue is also due to insufficient incentives for private companies to make the investments. This reflex by national governments, and also by the Commission, to start using public money to ensure the necessary investments, either to encourage companies to do it or to repair is often considered inadequate. One reason for such inadequacy, according to critics, is that the scale and size of investments needed are simply much too big and the risk of distorting the market and preventing the great majority of investment is too great.

Nevertheless, there are two examples from Hungary that suggest that public projects for infrastructure are not the wrong tool for ensuring necessary investment: One example is the Adriatic Oil Pipeline running from Hungary down to the Adriatic coast. Before this pipeline was built, due to an incentive from the Hungarian government, there was only one pipeline connecting Hungary to the Brotherhood pipeline from Russia. This pipeline was empty for almost 20 years. It is questionable who would build such a pipeline like the Adriatic Oil Pipeline on a private, risk/reward basis. Even at the time the investment took place, it was considered a 'wrong' investment. Today it is the only pipeline which saved the country from being blackmailed through oil supply coming to Hungary. It was a major security asset for the country.

The second example is the Austrian-Hungarian pipeline put in place 10-15 years ago. For 10-13 years, it was almost empty because Russian gas was cheaper. Now, it is 100 percent utilized because there is the business opportunity to bring cheap western European gas to the country. How would an open season have looked 15 years ago for the investment of that capacity? An open season might have been a failure for that investment but today seems to be a very valuable asset. Thus, how do we handle these issues?

Implementing the Third Package – Unbundling One of the key elements of the Third Energy Package is the requirement to unbundle. Once fully implemented by the Member States, unbundling might address well the problem of strategic underinvestment. The unbundling approach is considered an appropriate tool in this regard. For example, progressive unbundling will help to involve more companies that are actually interested in making sure that the necessary investments will take place on a commercial basis and will be market-driven. Ownership unbundling (rather than the independent transmission operator (ITO) or independent system operator (ISO) model) would be the best model since it guarantees complete independence and the business model is based on investing in infrastructure and operating that infrastructure. The 'half-way' models ITO and ISO are considered being not sustainable. Within a few years the EU might witness a move towards mergers, integration and regionalization of TSOs. These TSOs should be ownership unbundled.

The role of DG COMP. Finally, the lack of investment and/or the strategic underinvestment in some parts of Europe is mirrored in several cases DG COMP pursued against big incumbent companies. Reference has been made in these cases to 'strategic under-investment' referring to the infrastructure that could serve to protect national markets by not investing in new infrastructure and protecting the local market for local incumbents.

3. Experiences: two case studies

This section looks at significant experiences of Member States during the January 2009 crisis. By time of the crisis the amount and duration of disruption exceeded all planning assumptions. There was a 100 percent disruption for two weeks. Note that a similar supply situation had different consequences in the different affected Member States. There was no gas supply for industry for instance in Slovakia and Hungary. There was no gas for industry and only limited gas supply for households and district heating for instance in Bulgaria. Conversely, there was no noticeable effect for household and industrial gas customers for instance in Austria. Against such a background the question is why some countries managed the crisis much better than others. Looking at this question in greater depth, one needs to recall that at any given time during that gas crisis Europe had no shortage of gas. The gas simply was not where it was needed.

3.1 Solidarity during the 2009 January gas crisis – the case of Central and South-East Europe

Any attempt to understand what solidarity means cannot ignore the 2009 gas crisis. Mostly due to the asymmetries in network topology and gas supply sourcing, this crisis had a highly asymmetric impact on the EU gas economies. This asymmetry indicates a lack of interconnection and interconnectivity of the system. The problem was not a lack of gas in the EU, but rather, a lack of infrastructure: the existing infrastructure could not deliver the gas to those areas of Europe where it was mostly needed.

There were four different events that were related to solidarity and supply security during those almost three weeks back in 2009:

Event 1 During those weeks of crisis, additional shipments arrived to those markets with physical constraints and non-functional markets from Germany through Austria and from Hungary down to Serbia and Bosnia and Herzegovina. There are, therefore, very illustrative cases showing how the TSOs, after experimenting with reverse flows, and how multinational companies, having interest in different countries across the region, acted to help those countries in need.

The specific view regarding Austria shows that Austria had a well-functioning balancing market that was, besides crisis action plans and other government measures, responsible for good crisis management. When Russian supplies were lost, the balancing market prices increased to a notable extent. Then the other supply from storage operators, importers and producers reacted to that price increase and the Austrian balancing market could deliver to serve load immediately. The amount traded daily on the market reached the usual average monthly amount. In other words, it was possible to supply in one week the amount of gas that used to be supplied in one month. There was a natural and healthy market reaction to the loss of supply. This was not possible in Hungary, nor Serbia, nor in Bosnia and Herzegovina or Croatia, where markets and price mechanisms were incapable of playing a role in coping with the crisis because there was no functioning market. In this case E.ON played a prominent role, managing, together with the Austrian and Hungarian TSOs, to contract and ship additional gas into the affected countries. There was no price advantage exploited. Instead, reverse flow experiments by TSOs played a major role in that act and multinational gas companies played a major role in carrying out that act of solidarity. Note that it requires a complete change in the operation of the system to bring gas from, for instance, German storage sites down through Austria and Hungary to Serbia and Bosnia to accomplish this solidarity shipment of gas into the region. It is documented that, before the crisis, E.ON, at its headquarters in Essen, began setting up emergency plans defining how and what to do if the Russians closed the tap. It was already planning how to manage these shipments if the emergency came. Another example is RWE arranging supplies to the regions of the Czech Republic and Slovakia and managing finally to reverse flows on the Slovak-Czech interconnector around the end of the crisis, which allowed it to make shipments down and helping Slovakia. That was a prominent example of solidarity.

Event 2 is related to Hungary. During the crisis there has been discussion that Hungary should respond to the request of the Serbian Republic and Bosnia for solidarity shipments. The governments were asking Hungary because of its relatively abundant storage site. Those countries were asking for solidarity shipments due to their 100 percent dependence on Russian shipments. Finally, the Hungarian government and the company decided to provide these shipments without exploiting the price advantage. This led to the strange situation where Hungary was exporting to Serbia and Bosnia at the cost of the Hungarian customers: the supply to some Hungarian customers was curtailed while at the same time Hungary was shipping gas to consumers in Bosnia and Herzegovina. This made for a tough case. One argument was that the system operator and the regulator did not want to screw up the normative curtailment regime that Hungary had. It had a restriction regime in place between 7th and the 16th of January reducing 6-7 million cubic meters per day for large consumers. Because this was more than needed, part of it could be exported to Serbia and Bosnia. The regulator did not want to make a differentiation within that restriction category providing gas for some consumers and no gas for other consumers because of the potential of litigation after the crisis. There were no predefined liability rules for emergency situations. TSO nominations were in place in the country, so the TSO wanted to avoid the possibility of legal disputes after the crisis that also may have played a role in that act of solidarity.

Event 3 is related to Slovakia. The crisis led to strong political reactions at national level. It is about access to the Slovak storage capacity, which is substantial compared to the domestic consumption of Slovakia. During the crisis, access to Slovak storage capacity for cross border shipments by foreign players was possible but very much criticized after the crisis by the Slovak government. It has been criticized that during the crisis there was gas in storage in Slovakia, but Slovakian consumers did not get access to it because foreign players took the gas from storage and shipped it out of Slovakia. Storage assets are partially foreign-owned in Slovakia. In addition, foreign players booked a major part of the capacity. Access to storage did not work during the crisis. The government proposed to establish a wholesale and storage undertaking partly owned by the State. In addition, the case for a strategic gas storage site has been discussed. The Slovak Minister of Economy was referring to a full takeover of control of gas storage by the Slovak government. The Ministry of Economy would have the powers to suspend extraction capacities for customers outside Slovakia and use them preferentially for the country. A corresponding legislation was approved in February 2009.

Event 4 is the case of a 1.2 Bcm strategic storage site developed by Hungary with the original intention for crisis-only use and no Third Party Access (TPA). It is publically financed and the cost is recovered through regulated tariffs. It is an extremely expensive supply security measure opened in January 2009. Only the Energy Minister can grant access. There was a recent debate about the cost of the asset and the optimal size of a strategic reserve. A reduction of size from 1.2 Bcm down to 600 mcm is likely, allowing the rest to take part in gas market competition. The access during crisis is still pending. It should be a part of the risk assessment and emergency planning that is related to Regulation (EU) No 994/2010. The crisis led to significant policy reactions and investment in Hungary. As an example, at the end of 2010, i.e. within two years, there was a fifty-seven percent increase in underground storage capacity. The same accounts for the import pipeline capacity which has been increased by seventy-one percent, mostly from the Ukrainian side but also from the Croatian and Romanian interconnections that were put in place.

Lessons learnt out of these 4 illustrative events
• Well-functioning gas markets are prerequisite to manage crisis • Rules for TSO decisions on the spot need to be defined *ex antee* (liability, commercial settlements) • Common rules/ joint utilization for cross border access to storage

Regulation (EU) No 994/2010 reflects the first lesson when it is talking about solidarity. It is said that the internal gas market provides for the highest level of supply security if it is functional. The fact that those countries that were better connected to the German/Austrian markets such as the Czech Republic and Slovenia could manage the crisis without any customer curtailment demonstrates that the market integration really worked. This also means, in conclusion, that an enhanced integration is necessary. The Regulation then asks for mechanisms for prevention and disruption periods that are to be manifested in preventive and emergency plans. This is work in progress and it will be seen whether there will be any joint preventative and emergency action plans by Member States. Regional cooperation is a major field to put solidarity into practice. In response to the lessons learned during the crisis major areas for action – preventative and on spot – that can be defined are:

Market building and market integration might be the number one priority. Cross border and storage access rules should be there even for crisis situations, sending the message that when there is an emergency, market rules should remain in effect, as should access to cross-border capacities and storage. Integrated balancing zones are potential means by which to handle this issue on a more regional manner. Implementation of reverse flow options is crucial to make a foundation for future solidarity. There is, for example, a new interconnection between Hungary and Romania. It is only single directional at the moment. It should fall under the reverse flow obligation of the 2010 Regulation, although it is not sure yet whether Romania is in favor of letting any gas leave Romania for Hungary. It remains to be seen whether Romania and the Romanian gas TSO will ask for an exemption for the Hungarian/ Romanian interconnection in connection with the reverse flow obligation. If this should be the case, it might be seen as evidence of non-solidarity. Common infrastructure development projects are key to solidarity as well. Examples include the Hungarian/Slovakian interconnection, or the Czech/ Polish interconnection currently underway.

Definition of liability rules Moreover financial liability rules for not respecting contracts during emergencies should be defined. It is important that potential partners who might screw up former contracts during crisis times are explicitly liable for that behavior and know the precise scope of liability *ex ante*.

Joint prevention and emergency planning – In this regard, especially, demand side measure harmonization could be a cheap solution for the countries as well as the joint utilization of strategic storage sites. Doubts whether the Hungarian approach to develop the strategic storage is a sort of market distortion and might even have crowded out investment in other countries seem to be out of place. The boom in storage capacity increase was partially due to the 1.2 billion of strategic storage. At the same time, E.ON invested into commercial storage of the same size or even larger. In Hungary, there is good geology for underground storage. For Hungary, underground storage may be a good asset to sell in the regional context. If Europe will cooperate more effectively, cross-border access to pipelines will be regulated and the market integration will spread in the region.

3.2 The Belgian case

Belgium has a very special role in Northwestern Europe because it is the only big gas transit country. It is very well interconnected with other countries and that means that solidarity is key in some circumstances. There is no production in Belgium, but it has been importing for over 40 years. Supply disruption problems had never occurred. Security of supply is not an issue anymore. Diversity of supply has been a key policy objective for Belgium since the beginning and this goal has been reached.

Each of the 16 interconnection points with the UK, the Netherlands, Germany, Luxembourg and France represents a significant part of Belgian capacity demand. A very big diversion of flows is required in order to cooperate. But that makes potential volatility of flows quite huge. On top of that there is the East-West axis, which connects markets bi-directionally. The UK and continental markets are linked. The flows are according to the market prices in the UK (National Balancing Point (NBP)) and Belgium (Zeebrugge hub). There is a seasonal flow from the UK to Germany in summer and, in winter, gas flows back in the other direction. There is no visibility at all to what the UK actually stores in Germany. The only way one can derive data is through the flows. Everything happens through the market signals, through prices.

What is the TSO experience of solidarity? TSOs collaborate with all their neighboring TSOs. TSOs cooperate for network development, for normal operations but also for unplanned operations when something goes wrong in order to find the best solution.

Looking specifically at the Belgian experience, the picture regarding solidarity was much clearer in the past. Transit and transport were completely separate. For example there was a clear distinction between flows for domestic transport and transit. Downstream countries could rely on transit routes without any interference resulting from a situation in the transit country. If there was for instance a problem in Belgium the flow to France could not be interrupted. As a consequence, and big disadvantage, the markets are closed, consisting of adjacent Member States with "dedicated" infrastructure. Today, with liberalized markets the gas can go from one country to the other. That means also that any distinction is blurred. It is not clear whether the pipeline going to France is used for France or Belgium or Germany. Now, with the advantage of competition in gas and more market players, prices are on the downswing. However, France cannot rely anymore on the pipeline capacity. That will be fully working with market based solutions. The key issue for the TSO now is to manage the complexity with all the diverse interests of the market participants, particularly since the legal and regulatory framework is not yet in place. Currently Member States are working on impact assessments. Afterwards the same needs to be done at regional and EU level. One problem might be that the supply standard is much weaker than the infrastructure standard and that could lead to a situation where the right incentives on the commodity side are not on the same level as on the capacity side.

Flows in Belgium in January 2009 – What happened in January 2009 in practice regarding the flows in Belgium? Demand was very high in Belgium due to low temperature. It was the same in other countries such as in France and Eastern Europe. The flow from the UK increased nearly to maximum capacity. This gas from the UK was mainly going to Germany. A lot was also going to France, due to the fact that France had lost its supplies from Russia and France's storage was not enough. The January 2009 experience proved that market-based solutions worked in Northwestern Europe. A redirection of flows took place from West to East. Shippers rebalanced their portfolio according to the source availability. Spot prices did not increase significantly. At the beginning of the crisis they remained quite high but sometimes they were lower and then higher again. Even after the crisis there was the same level of price as at the beginning of the crisis. Reason for the price increase was a combination of low temperature and higher than expected demand in the UK. Then there is some price difference needed to bring some price back to Europe.

The lesson learned from this time is, above all, that a clear definition of responsibilities; a clear regulatory and legal framework is needed. There was also a need for more transparency. What was also important is that an EU crisis has to be dealt with on EU level. Regional crises are dealt with on the regional level. But this is adequately dealt with in the 2010/944 Regulation. The preventative part, the risk assessment, preventative action and emergency plan need further work.

Lessons learnt
• **Market-based solutions work in NW Europe** – Redirection of flows from West to East – Shippers rebalanced their portfolio according to source availability – Spot prices: no strong increase experienced • **Improvements necessary:** – Better definition of roles and responsibilities – Improve coordination across Member States – Need to improve prevention part: risk assessment (supply disruption scenarios), capacity standard (N-1 criteria), supply standard

4. Solidarity tools

This section aims at reviewing the tools that shall provide for solidarity. Solidarity is about providing something that the market does not provide by itself. It is about having a Member State step in to help its neighbour. It is about giving the right incentives or even enforce industry players in general to act in a way which is not necessarily in their self-interest but for the interest of the whole Union.

The solidarity concept has been introduced as a political concept. Industry and business that are supposed to implement it sometimes find it difficult to understand what it means concretely and how to deal with it. A well-functioning gas market shall be the best guarantee for solidarity because it should create all the liquidity needed. However, for instance, in order to build the infrastructure necessary to provide the basis for solidarity the EU may need a different investment framework. The market alone does not always provide incentives for investments used and needed for solidarity.

4.1 Solidarity in the law

Common interests result in solidarity. Note that the 'common interest' is greater than the sum of individual interests. According to Max Weber, solidarity is a prerequisite to law. The people accept power, intervention from above, only if they sense that they are in a community of solidarity. If there is solidarity and the laws have been adopted by the rules of that solidarity community, according to the rules, then the laws will be accepted. Once there is the law it contributes to solidarity because it creates credibility and confidence in the system of solidarity. The law channels and consolidates the will to live in solidarity. So solidarity is a prerequisite to legislation but the legislation also contributes to solidarity. The problem is that in the EU it was not exactly like that. While at the beginning there was a sense of solidarity that was the cold war and a feeling together, such feeling of solidarity has dissolved. The individual citizen does not always recognize benefits. Then, the EU law did not clearly contribute to solidarity. It frequently looks bureaucratic and above all appears to contradict the interests of the single Member State.

Solidarity, which is not a part of the Treaty of Rome, was first mentioned in the 1992 Maastricht Treaty. Today, the Treaty on the EU (which results from the Lisbon Treaty) calls for solidarity between people. The Union shall promote economic, social and territorial cohesion and solidarity among its members. Cohesion does not mean homogeneity but it means cohesion in diversity, solidarity in diversity.

Then, we have the Treaty of the Functioning of the European Union, the TFEU. Solidarity is mentioned there 22 times, two times that are of interest for the specific energy context. It has been added to the already existing Article 103, and most important, in the new energy chapter, Article 194, speaking about the pursuit of EU energy policy in a "spirit of solidarity." Note that security of supply was already in the initial draft of the EU convention while solidarity (and interconnection) were added at the last moment at the Lisbon conference, not in the original drafts of the convention or the intergovernmental conferences before. Although the provision speaks "only" about a "spirit of solidarity" it is important from a legal point of view. It is not just a possibility to do something, but an obligation. There is an obligation flowing from Article 194 to pursue solidarity actively.

Negative and positive tools – Looking at the tools of solidarity there are negative tools and positive tools. A negative tool is a policy action by the European Commission that implements the basic freedoms. It is about the internal market. In theory we have solidarity already enshrined in the basic freedoms of the internal market: the free flow of goods and services, etc. No Member State may block the border; there must be no restriction on flow. This means solidarity. The first check was in the oil crisis 1974. The European Commission had to start infringement procedures against 8 of 9 Member States because they had put exports of petroleum products to other Member States under a system of automatic licenses. Eight Member States gave in. This is one example of enforced solidarity.

However, it is not sufficient that the internal market simply "works." It only truly works if some positive tools are added. A positive tool is a legislative action. That is why we have the Internal Energy Market Directives, including the unbundling regime as introduced by the Third Package. There is a long list of public interests of consumers, of public interests of small and medium enterprises and so on. There are the Directives on the stocks in order to avoid the free riders problems. All of these positively address solidarity. A positive tool is also about infrastructure, internal and external. It also helps to foster the unbundling mechanisms.

4.2 Investment needs

According to the Commission's recent proposal on a Regulation on guidelines for trans-European energy infrastructure [COM(2011) 658]: „The investment costs (…) shall (…) be paid for by network users through tariffs for network access" in *Member States to which the project provides a net positive impact, (Art. 13 (1)). Article 13 thu*s incorporates the principle of fiscal equivalence in the sense that the beneficiary has to pay for an investment. The question then arises of "Who is the *beneficiary* of energy infrastructure"? To highlight the difficulties connected to answering this question one might refer again to the case of the Russian Ukraine gas crisis. To avoid a replay, investments are needed in Western parts of Europe. The beneficiaries will be in the Eastern parts of Europe. Thus, when it comes to the principle of fiscal equivalence one must deal with both parties.

Moreover, the strategic concerns of governments in connection with infrastructure decisions need to be taken into account. Governments have preferences for specific infrastructure sites due to foreign relation aspects with other EU Member States or with non-EU states. If the government is correct in making this strategic decision, who is the beneficiary of this infrastructure site? It is not only the users of energy. Foreign relations benefits must also be kept in mind. This may open the floor for some taxpayer's money on infrastructure decisions.

In addition, the common goals concerning energy use qualify as benefits. If all Member States must comply with the rules of the EU's climate protection and renewables policy and energy infrastructure plays a role in complying with these rules, then all Member States are affected by energy infrastructure decisions. The principle of fiscal equivalence is correct from an economic point of view. However, unavoidably there exists some leeway politically in the context of the beneficiary pays principle and it is impossible to get rid of that.

According to the European Commission, € 1 trillion needs to be invested by 2020 for the entire EU energy network. In the business as usual scenario there will be a 100 billion Euro financing gap. Who pays? According to the Commission and the EU Council, the "user pays" principle applies in conjunction with regulated tariffs (see Article 13 of the proposed Regulation). There might be some risk sharing aspects here. Therefore, the Commission proposed the Connecting Europe Facility. This might be an instrument to encourage investors to risk their money as this money would be backed by funds from the EIB and the EU budget. If infrastructure cannot be financed through regular user fees but it is important in terms of solidarity in a narrower sense then taxpayers will pay their part of the bill. Maybe the Baltic States and the connection of those States with the EU energy system may be an example for that.

4.3 The Infrastructure Package

The Regulation on the energy infrastructures and the Connecting Europe Facility are measures that address *ex ante* solidarity, to ensure that the EU infrastructure is fit and in good condition in case there is a future crisis. The background is, as discussed above, that a lack of coordination of infrastructure prevented the effective mitigation of the 2009 January gas crisis. The aim of the energy infrastructure Regulation is to provide policy and regulatory certainty of the market to be able to deliver the necessary investments, first by 2020, but also in the long term. It is about strengthening the markets' capacity to deliver what is needed in order to address crisis that may come. 12 priority corridors and thematic areas have been identified for the 2020 and long-term period. Four of them are in gas. There is the Baltic region, North-South connections in Western Europe, North-South connections in central Eastern and South Eastern Europe and the Southern gas corridor. In gas, the focus is on high pressure transmission, underground storage and LNG, Compressed Natural Gas (CNG) plus management systems, i.e. other equipment that is necessary.

The new legislation needs to be seen in the light of today's situation. Today, there is the Trans-European Network policy, which identifies various types of priority projects. The respective Annexes contain 550 projects in total. In other words, there are no priorities. Such a list in a legal text has proven to be very cumbersome. It cannot easily be changed in the sense of being adapted. The benefit to such a list is that it gives the Member States and the EU Parliament the opportunity to include all possible and impossible projects in one place in order not to please anyone; however, the new approach is to completely change this, i.e. to not have project lists, but to have a process of ranking projects.

4.3.1 Projects of Common Interest (PCI)

This process of identification of projects is embedded in the 3rd Energy Package's instruments and institutions/organizations. It is intended to use a regional approach as a tool not as a purpose itself. The regional approach is meant as a stepping-stone towards a European approach. In this regional approach, TSOs, or other project promoters shall be brought together with the regulators and the Member States' authorities. The aim in this regional context is to build a consensus on what is needed: where the bottlenecks are, what the priorities are and to come up with a proposal for a regional list of projects that would receive a label of common interest. The identification of these projects in the regional context would not be based solely on a discussion but also on technical criteria aimed at identifying, first, the European ideal value of these projects and also how they serve the European policy objectives. Before a project will be considered as being of any common European interest it would need to demonstrate its benefits for at least two Member States. It is the minimum to be of European common interest.

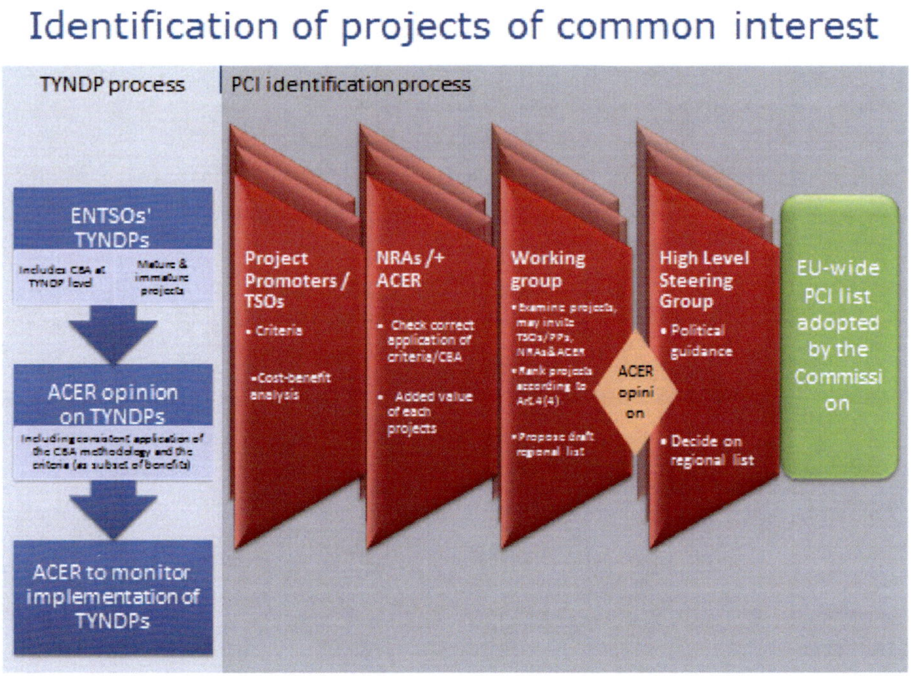

Source: European Commission, DG ENER

The benefits of qualifying as Projects of Common Interest (PCI) would be acceleration of the permit granting procedures, certain regulatory treatment, and incentives and financing. Projects shall benefit from a process with for instance a three years' time limit for the permit granting decision. The regulatory framework will provide for an energy-system wide cost-benefit analysis. This is interesting especially in cases of projects where the costs and benefits are asymmetrically attributed between the counties or the different players. The beneficiaries in country A could or should contribute financially to the investments in country B. Gas is a very typical example of such a case. Examples are the reverse flow projects that the EU has already been financing under the recovery plan.

The beneficiary-based principle, the cross-border cost allocation (as it is called in the Regulation), should be based on an agreed methodology on how to measure and how to assess and how to value the costs and benefits. There, the mandate is with the ENTSOs to work on a methodology that will then be subject to public consultation before it is adopted. The NRAs would have a strong role in this process. They would have to agree jointly on cost allocation.

In case of no agreement, ACER would decide. Moreover the Regulation would require the NRAs to grant appropriate incentives on a case-by-case basis to address abnormal risks.

As said, another benefit is on financing. The Connecting Europe Facility allocated 9.12 bn Euros to energy. Of course, this is the starting point of the discussion and it remains to be seen where the budget discussion will take us. The period covered is 2014 up to 2020. Not all PCIs would have access to direct financing. All PCIs that get the label except oil would be eligible for grants for studies that allow to shape the project and assess its feasibility or environmental impacts. Only in exceptional cases would projects be eligible for grants for works. In such cases the cost-benefit analysis would have to demonstrate that there are positive externalities e.g. innovative technology, regional or EU-wider security of supply. The business plan would also have to demonstrate that the project cannot go ahead without some public support and these two assessments, the cost benefit analysis and the business plan assessment, would also need to go through the regulators and get their endorsement. Only after this process could a project be eligible for direct funding for grants. Finally, there are some safeguards in the Regulation that are expected to prevent the EU from pouring money on projects that do not need to be undertaken.

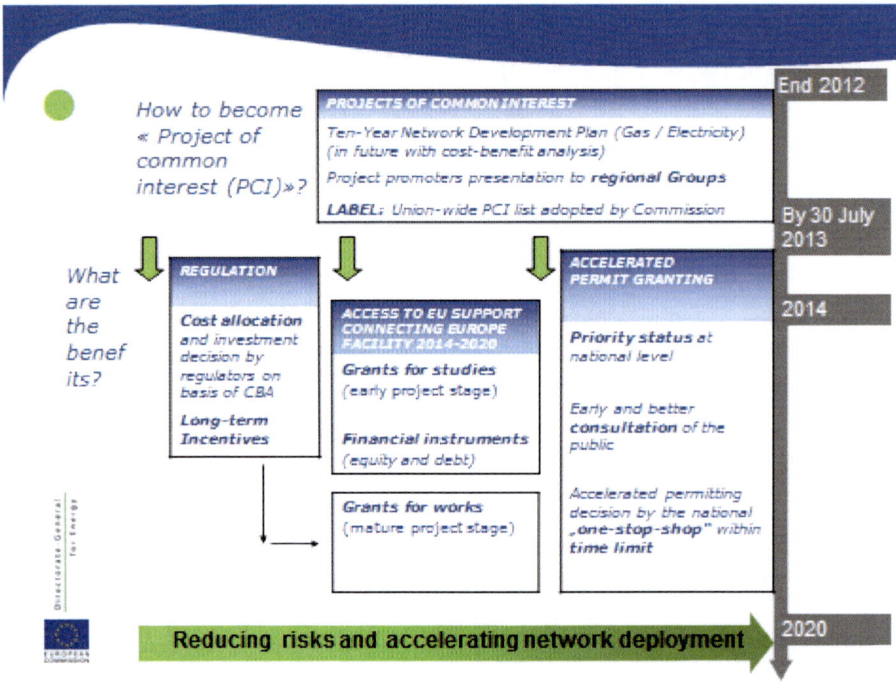

Source: European Commission, DG ENER, March 2012

4.3.2 System wide cost benefit analysis

When it comes to cross border, the method referred to above means sufficient geographical coverage to be able to assess the cost and benefits sufficiently, so that the regulators can then take a decision on that basis. Thus, at that stage, a system wide or cross-sector cost benefit analysis is not intended. However, in the legal text there is also an article whereby the ENTSOs are asked again to work on a joint gas/electricity modeling that is to allow for longer term forecasting and calculation. It is not to ask the ENTSOs, or anybody else, to take decisions on the basis of cost allocation. For that, we need a more local and short-term perspective.

Solidarity beyond EU borders? Neighbouring countries are included when there is a 'corridor logic' in the sense that there is a connection between an EU country and a neighbouring country. In this case not only just the neighbouring country is included. Solidarity applies here "as far as it needs to go," i.e. in gas, all the way to the source of the gas. Exceptionally, the financing could then be extended for these investments but these projects would have to have the label of PCIs and would then have to be addressed in the regional discussions. Thus, "neighboring countries" include, for instance, countries like Turkey or Bulgaria, as well as the Mediterranean countries.

4.4 Short excursus: the Baltic Energy Market Interconnection Plan

One example of solidarity put into practice is the Baltic Energy Market Interconnection Plan (BEMIP), which originates from seven countries located around the Baltic Sea. The region is fragmented into three unconnected sub regions: Denmark and Sweden; Poland; Lithuania, Latvia, Estonia and Finland, isolated from the EU transmission system. Almost 100 percent of the gas currently imported into the region is sourced from Russia (not including, Denmark and Sweden). The national markets have growth potential, but because of the fragmentation and the size, the region has limited attraction for upstream players and traders. The presence of different market rules in every country (capacity allocation methods, contractual conditions, etc.) is a further obstacle. Integration and diversification is required to create a competitive and liquid market in the region with increased security of energy supply in the long term. There is no domestic production in the region except for Poland (including unconventional potential) and Denmark (depleting fields). The EU has included the BEMIP among its energy infrastructure priorities. Seven

TSOs are currently involved in the work on the regional plan, the BEMIP GRIP to identify the most relevant initiatives that could merit EU economic, regulatory and legislative support.

5. Outlook and conclusion

Solidarity has proven to be a missing point in European energy policy in the past. Europe has experienced a European gas market mainly based on national politics with the "national champion" being responsible for securing the supply of each country independently.

The January 2009 gas crisis was only one catalyst that led to making solidarity a priority rather than a slogan in the gas security of supply context. Today, besides the fact that the basic freedoms of the internal market, such as the free flow of goods and services, etc., are guarantors of solidarity and the more specific recent enshrinement of the obligation of the Member States to act in a "spirit of solidarity" – referring to the new energy chapter, Article 194 TFEU – solidarity in gas is translated into concrete action mainly by means of the secondary law.

It is, first of all, the gas security of supply Regulation (EU) No 994/2010 that brings a solid base for organizing and managing unforeseen supply interruptions on a short-term basis. Especially for gas, with its major differences in gas supply structures in the EU, the Regulation is the EU-wide solidarity instrument in times of gas shortages. It is not only the 2009 gas crisis, but also earlier and later developments, continuing as recently as winter 2011, that are giving important experiences for further refining and improving procedures under the Regulation. This articulation and lessons-learned program should continue, without forgetting that each crisis has unique characteristics and is, therefore, unpredictable. Certainly, there are issues that still need to be resolved or are still missing in the Regulation (EU) No 994/2010, one example being public service obligations. In particular, the way in which we must manage a public service obligation that is in collision with solidarity. For instance, France has a level of public service obligation higher than that in the 2010/944 Regulation. That means consumers are more protected than the minimum level set up by the Regulation. During a gas crisis, what is the right way of dealing with two contradicting obligations? To lighten temporarily this obligation in order to allow France to respect its obligation towards all the European countries in gas needs?

A second legal tool providing the prerequisite for solidarity being infrastructure and interconnections is the infrastructure package. The Regulation on the energy infrastructures and the Connecting Europe Facility are measures that address *ex ante* solidarity, to ensure that the EU infrastructure is fit and in good condition in case there should be a future crisis. The new infrastructure package is actually, finally after many years, trying to address the need to invest, by looking at the common European interests and not just the interests of the private companies or even the blind interest of countries.

Another precondition for solidarity is transparency. In this respect, the increased efforts in EU foreign energy relations, most recently with the proposal for a Transparency Decision for intergovernmental agreements, is a promising step in the right direction. The EU is on a way towards solidarity *ex ante* when it comes to institution building for crisis prevention, as well as for ensuring crisis management on the spot in a spirit of solidarity.

CHAPTER IV

CONCLUSION AND RECOMMENDATIONS

Jacques de Jong (CIEP)
Manfred Hafner (FEEM)
Jean-Michel Glachant (EUI)
Nicole Ahner (EUI)
Simone Tagliapietra (FEEM)

Discussions and reflections reported from the various workshops held under this project have developed into the following concluding ideas and recommendations for a new EU gas security of supply architecture. These are further summarized and elaborated as input for the policy-discussions that are developing in 2012 at the different EU levels.

Secure and reliable external supply flows to EU markets

Assessing security in the supply/demand balance requires a clear view on the EU's market needs. Security of demand is a prerequisite for security of supply and *vice versa*. Although high levels of uncertainty will have to be recognized, it is expected that natural gas will continue to play an important - and even increasing - role in the EU fuel mix for the decades to come. While natural gas was considered to be the "*fuel of choice*" for some time, it could become the "*fuel of consequence*" especially where alternatives for gas in power generation are facing specific problems of their own. The EU's developing gas demand in the medium and longer terms is largely based on the role that market participants are seeing for this fuel in the overall energy mix. This role is broadly based on the energy policies that the EU and the Member States are defining and implementing and the way in which market parties are applying and implementing the use of gas and the resulting demand.

Energy demand, gas demand and the demand for other energy fuels and sources are basically long-term issues. Accordingly is the policy basis. While the EU has agreed on an energy policy framework for the period up to 2020, policies for the period beyond 2020 are still under consideration. It would be very useful to approach these policies and the resulting role for gas with the view in mind of giving the levels of demand security that would help suppliers to offer the required levels of supply security. In that context, the "golden age for gas" as predicted globally by the International Energy Agency (IEA) could emerge also for the EU. For this to happen, two main conditions need to be taken into account: the development of a clear signal from the EU on its needs for gas and the further deployment of cost effective means for capturing and storing carbon emissions.

Another issue which over the last years has transformed global gas markets and will continue playing an increasingly important role is shale gas. In fact, over the last few years shale gas has experienced in the US a massive development representing today about two thirds of the country's domestic gas production. This "shale gas revolution" has radically changed the global natural gas environment with impacts also for Europe as important new Liquefied Natural Gas (LNG) supplies originally destined to the US market have reached North-West Europe therefore uncoupling spot gas prices from long-term oil indexed gas prices. Due to the shale gas development, gas prices in the US have dramatically fallen over the last years. This new environment provides today great expectations among American leaders for a new American industrial and economic renaissance. Several LNG export projects have been proposed in the US to take advantage of the important price differential with Europe (three to four times higher) and Asia (six-seven times higher). However, there are strong political hurdles for significant US LNG export quantities as this would increase the domestic gas prices. We therefore do not expect important LNG supplies from the US to Europe. With regard to the European domestic dimension, there is presently no production of shale gas in Europe. Poland and France are thought to have large shale-gas resources (together with Norway, Ukraine, Sweden, Denmark and the United Kingdom). However, developing most of these resources appears to be problematic in the EU due to environmental and regulatory issues as well as missing public acceptance. In fact, some European countries like France have for the time being banned shale gas production. There may be some potential in Poland due to the country's strong willingness to become more independent from Russian gas.

Assessing the major existing and potential external supply sources for the EU, Norway, Russia, the Middle East and North Africa (MENA)-region and the Caspian Basin are the determinant factors for the EU's gas security of supply chessboard.

Norway has always been a reliable supplier, but some concerns are emerging about its longer-term supply capabilities. Significant gas discoveries have not been done in the last decade and different studies are indicating a production peak around 2020.

Russia, the largest resource holder in the world, will continue to be the EU's main external supply source. The EU and Russia have on this point an intractable interdependency. Hence the EU-Russia Energy dialogue (or any other appropriate instrument) should remain and be further developed as a fundamental aspect of any EU gas supply security architecture. Energy supply and demand strategies, developing upstream potentials, coordination of R&D in relation to supply and transportation, policy discussions on market designs and business models are among the prime issues to be put on the dialogue agenda's.

The MENA-region as such is holding large resource potentials, both conventional and unconventional. Domestic consumption in the region is however growing rapidly, largely driven by the power sector, even leading to gas shortages in some countries. Export potentials to the EU therefore are not to be overestimated. EU-relations with the region do bring substantial win-win potentials, both in conventional energy but more specifically in renewable energy sources. The EU should therefore move in the direction of building and further enhancing new and existing institutional frames for political and economic cooperation, where energy could be one of the key vectors on which mutual trust and confidence could successfully be further developed.

The Caspian Basin with its considerable amount of proven gas reserves could be considered as a new frontier for the EU's gas supplies, further diversifying its resource basis. Direct exports to the EU via the Southern Corridor concept would however bring numerous geopolitical and infrastructural hurdles that are still being explored with the governments that are both directly and indirectly involved. The European Commission is being engaged in several dialogues at technical and political levels. The success for the EU in achieving a viable flow of gas through the Southern Corridor to EU markets seems to require effective and reliable mechanisms for the EU to speak "with one voice" and to act and deliver accordingly.

EU gas infrastructures to and through EU markets: EU challenges and external relations

Bringing gas to EU- markets is largely coming via pipelines from the North, the North-East, the East, the South-East and the South. Policy attention is largely focusing on the South Eastern Corridor that should bring gas from the Caspian Basin, and on the South Stream project, bringing Russian supplies. On the Caspian issue, a number of more or less competing projects are on the table. It may be expected that in the course of 2012 further decisions will be made as to the infrastructures to let Caspian gas entering EU markets.

South Stream is a different story, opening a third outlet for Russian supplies in addition to the northern route via the new Nord Stream pipelines and the already existing roads from Russia via Ukraine and Belorussia. There are however some differences between Nord Stream and South Stream, when it comes to ownership[15], but more importantly when it comes to project definition. North Stream is landing on the EU-border, where it is further connected to other pipelines. South Stream is bringing gas through the EU, with a number of exits in its transiting EU and non-EU markets. This brings a different and still pending regulatory framework, especially in relation to the EUs Third Energy Package. In addition to that, the geopolitical dimension in relation to both the Ukrainian route and the competitive position vis-à-vis Caspian supplies brings further complexities. The next 1 to 2 years will probably be decisive for the whole South-Eastern Corridor and its gas supplies to the South Eastern EU market.

When it comes to the internal EU infrastructures for gas, the European Network of Transmission System Operators for Gas (ENTSO-G) has a leading role to play. It is in the framework of its new ten-year network development plans (TYNDP) where coordinated network development planning at EU and regional levels will be done. Financing and the relevant regulatory EU and national regimes are critical factors, not only when it comes to risk/reward balances, but also for the various access conditions and capacity

15 NS has a 51% Gazprom-stake, with some major EU industry stakes for the other 49%, whereas SS is a 50/50 venture between Gazprom and (other) EU partners.

allocation mechanisms. National regulators and the new ACER will be very instrumental in this regard. Similar issues are playing a role in the context of developing storage capacity and receiving terminals for LNG. All these issues are not only relevant for the TSOs and the shippers they are servicing, but also to a large extent for the EUs external suppliers, as the regulatory context will be a critical factor in assessing the overall business cases for securing existing and new supplies on a long-term basis.

The regulatory risk as it is perceived by the gas industry, the TSOs, the suppliers, the producers inside and outside the EU, will bring a major challenge to regulators and policy makers. The Third Energy Package is bringing a huge and ambitious regulatory agenda for a wide variety of intra-EU network access and capacity use issues that will further shape the internal EU gas market. Its Network Codes and underlying Framework Guidelines need to strike a fair and effective balance between the regulatory designs and the role that markets are allowed to play. Issues such as crossing border capacity allocation and congestion management and their impact on commodity markets and maybe forthcoming (pipeline) capacity markets, together with issues around transmission pricing, wholesale markets, spot markets, market hubs and their markers for market liquidity and price alignments, allowing regional differences wherever feasible, will be determinant factors for maintaining, developing and securing competitive gas supplies to EU consumers.

It will be quite clear that all these issues have to be seen in the context of changing market conditions, both within the EU and in the more global context of evolving international gas markets. Within the EU, the role of gas in the energy equation will be changing, due to the EUs ambitious sustainability agenda and the increasing share that intermittent renewable energy sources will play in the power generation fuel mix. Gas for power will increase, especially in a flexible way, transforming gas more and more into a peak-load fuel, with all sorts of consequences for the underlying business and market models and calls on infrastructure capacities. This will all have impacts on the (continuing) attractiveness of EU markets for external gas suppliers. Developing, designing, interpreting and applying these new regulatory frameworks require therefore close and transparent consultations with all stakeholders inside and outside the EU. Decision making by the relevant EU authorities therefore require striking a fair balance between the internal policy agenda and the external policy dimensions. The new Architecture should reflect this balance.

Infrastructures and the issue of internal solidarity

Solidarity has proven to be a missing point in European energy policy in the past. Europe has experienced a European gas market mainly based on national politics with the "national champion" being responsible for securing the supply of each country independently.

The January 2009 gas crisis was only one catalyst that led to making solidarity a priority rather than a slogan in the gas security of supply context. Today, besides the fact that the basic freedoms of the internal market, such as the free flow of goods and services, etc., are guarantors of solidarity and the more specific recent enshrinement of the obligation of the Member States to act in a "spirit of solidarity" – referring to the new energy chapter, Article 194 TFEU – solidarity in gas is translated into concrete action mainly by means of the secondary law.

It is, first of all, the gas security of supply Regulation (EU) No 994/2010 that brings a solid base for organizing and managing unforeseen supply interruptions on a short-term basis. Especially for gas, with its major differences in gas supply structures in the EU, the Regulation is the EU-wide solidarity instrument in times of gas shortages. It is not only the 2009 gas crisis, but also earlier and later developments, continuing as recently as winter 2011, that are giving important experiences for further refining and improving procedures under the Regulation. This articulation and lessons-learned program should continue, without forgetting that each crisis has unique characteristics and is, therefore, unpredictable. Certainly, there are issues that still need to be resolved or are still missing in the Regulation, one example being public service obligations. In particular, the way in which we must manage a public service obligation that is in collision with solidarity. For instance, France has a level of public service obligation higher than that in the 2010/944 Regulation. That means consumers are more protected than the minimum level set up by the Regulation. During a gas crisis, what is the right way of dealing with two contradicting obligations? To lighten temporarily this obligation in order to allow France to respect its obligation towards all the European countries in gas needs?

A second legal tool providing the prerequisite for solidarity being infrastructure and interconnections is the European Energy Infrastructure Package. The Regulation on the energy infrastructures and the Connecting Europe Facility are measures that address *ex ante* solidarity, to ensure that the EU infrastructure is fit and in good condition in case there should be a future crisis. The new infrastructure package is actually, finally after many years, trying to address the need to invest, by looking at the common European interests and not just the interests of the private companies or even the blind interest of countries.

Another precondition for solidarity is transparency. In this respect, the increased efforts in EU foreign energy relations, most recently with the proposal for a Transparency Decision for intergovernmental agreements, is a promising step in the right direction. The EU is on a way towards solidarity *ex ante* when it comes to institution building for crisis prevention, as well as for ensuring crisis management on the spot in a spirit of solidarity.

The new architecture: recommendations for a new approach

It would seem quite clear that securing supplies needs to be balanced with securing demand, and *vice versa*. The EU's developing gas demand in the medium and longer terms is largely based on the role that market participants are seeing for this fuel in the overall energy mix. This role is broadly the result of the energy policies that the EU and the Member States are defining and implementing. Energy demand, gas demand and the demand for other energy fuels and sources are basically long-term issues. Again, and so is the policy basis. As it is clear that the EU has agreed an energy policy framework for the period up to 2020, that is implemented at national levels and that for the period beyond 2020 these policies are under consideration, it would be very useful to approach the issue for a "new architecture" with these timeframes in mind.

For the period up to 2020, energy policy has decided on the role of renewable energy sources (RES) in the fuel mix, which gives some indication for the role of gas. With the increasing role of RES and maybe other non-fossil fuels for the period beyond 2020, the role of gas in the mix and more precisely the role of gas in the system becomes more important, exciting and less predictable. Important in the way that new and continuing supply arrangements will have to be made, both in terms of commodities and in terms of infrastructure capacity. Exciting, as the role of gas in power generation will change, due to its potential role of becoming a "flexibility fuel" in relation to the increase of intermittent energy sources, and hence the need for changing structures in market and regulatory designs, including prices, business models and infrastructure access conditions.

A very clear vision at EU level on these changes would therefore be very appropriate and should form an integral part of a new Architecture. The forthcoming discussions on the EU's Road Maps 2050 are presenting useful opportunities. Such a view could also give a clear signal to the upstream sector in the value chain, both within the EU but more importantly for the EU's external suppliers. This view could be seen as a basis for further developing, focusing and articulating the EU's external energy relations, energy diplomacy and policy in building secure and reliable relations with the EU's main gas suppliers and transport and transit routes.

For the period up to 2020, the policy agenda is focusing on the completion of the internal gas market design and the conditions for incentivizing the timely development of the necessary infrastructures. For these issues the speedy implementation of the Third Energy Package is critical, together with the timely decisions on the actions proposed in the new Infrastructure Regulation. A number of relevant issues are still pending, and it would be appropriate as well to clear them up without delay in order to give more clarity to all market parties in the value chain, including the EU's external suppliers.

A new EU Architecture for securing the EU's gas supply basis in the medium and longer terms should very well reflect the issues mentioned above. Special attention should be given to the 2050 Energy Road Map, as the policy discussions therein could be considered the global and integrated EU view on the longer-term energy mix with due regard to the transition towards a low-carbon energy economy. In addition, policy discussion and implementation are also relevant for gas supply security in the context of the EU's external energy policy. As a third consideration, the more medium-term agenda of "completing" the EU's internal gas market shall be mentioned.

With respect to the new architecture, it is strongly recommended to make a distinction between a longer-term focus, i.e. on the post 2020 period and a shorter/medium term focus, i.e. on the period up to 2020. For both periods it is recommended to define a clear and articulated policy vision.

The long-term vision

The long-term vision should cover three specific policy chapters: the role of gas in the energy fuel mix and energy system, the EU external energy policy focus and the EU internal gas market.

The role of gas

Security of supply and security of demand are two sides of the same coin. Building market confidence in the long-term is essential for both upstream and downstream investments and market signals. The EU should therefore develop a clear vision of the role it sees for gas in its global energy mix as part of the 2050 Roadmap. A choice should be made whether gas will (again) be a "fuel of destination", i.e. the fuel that gives in the medium and longer-term the most cost-effective and sustainable solution? Or will gas rather be considered as a "fuel of transition", i.e. the primary fuel that would help the EU on its road towards the carbon-free energy economy? Or, finally, will gas be considered as a "fuel of consequence", i.e. the fallback option should other options fail to deliver at the necessary times?

In any scenario on the role of gas in the energy system, the interaction between the gas and power sectors will need to grow dramatically. That would mean that gas demand would become more and more a function of the power generating systems, due to its large advantages as a flexible fuel. In addition, new innovative concepts of gas-to-power and power-to-gas interactions, including the application of electrolysis and storage technologies, will bring further options for the use of gas in the energy system. This changing role of gas will have no doubt dramatic consequences for the use of the gas-infrastructures (transmission and storage), with changing business models and increasing spot-oriented intra-EU trade. Market designs and regulatory designs will have to be reconsidered and the interaction between the power market and the various fuel markets, including the carbon market will increase as well. If Carbon Capture and Storage (CCS) is to be applied at larger scales, fine-tuning between the gas and power chains with the carbon chain would become a further challenge. A new gas supply architecture should reflect on these developments in order to enhance supplier confidence and consumer needs.

The external energy policy focus

External energy relations at the EU level, especially when external gas supplies are involved, should be built upon the vision mentioned in the first paragraph, and should lead to specific strategies for the EU's main suppliers. Taking due account of the developing global gas markets, focus should be put on, respectively, Norway, Russia, the Mediterranean region and the Caspian

Basin. For each of these, it would be appropriate to create a specific mechanism for periodic discussion, review and institutionalized approaches regarding gas supplies and related relevant policy issues.

As examples, the northern dimension could include the development of market structures and business models and could also give due account on the role of hydro as a storage option for managing intermittent energy sources, as well as the schemes for deploying large scale CCS. The eastern dimension should focus on the issue of mutual "win-win" schemes for applying reciprocity criteria in both the upstream and downstream segments of the value-chain. Equally important would be the issues regarding East-West transit-lines on the way to and through EU-markets, and eventually, the enhancement of the early warning systems in the case of supply interruptions.

The southern dimension could focus in a broader way on economic cooperation, including energy issues. Changing geo-political structures in the region might bring new opportunities for using the wide variety of EU instruments. Global political cooperation in the Mediterranean region, including on renewable energy such as the Desertec project and the relating Medgrid or Medreg initiatives might bring new momentum. The SE-EU dimension and its strategic energy pathways between the East and the South would bring further options for the EU, building, where necessary, on the Energy Community Treaty-framework, and could also include the ways and means of innovative gas purchasing schemes.

The internal EU gas market

The EU should strive to remain, for all external suppliers and for all of the three possible visions on the role of gas, an attractive market for suppliers. The internal market model should reflect, therefore, the changing market structures and conditions that will need to develop from the broader vision of the role of gas. For instance, the emergence of gas as a fuel for delivering flexibility and back-up in the increasingly RES-dominated power systems may have serious consequences for the prevailing gas market and regulatory designs. As part of the architecture, the EU should consider redefining its vision on the internal gas market, and remaining open to suggestions from its main external suppliers.

This changing role of gas will have a particularly precise and challenging impact regarding issues that go beyond national authorities and policy-making: short-term and spot trades will need to increase to manage flexible market demand; cross-border exchanges will further develop; and cross-border arbitrages in the gas/electricity/carbon market dimensions will have to develop (relying more frequently on short-term capacity requirements in pipelines and interconnections, with resulting capacity (under)use and allocations). Transits will be an expanded, normal way of moving gas through EU-markets, and infrastructure access and pricing will need to accommodate these flows. Storage will become more important, managing seasonal variations as well as much shorter-term daily or weekly variations.

For these and other issues, effective cross-border regulatory oversight and designs will need to be developed further, perhaps more on regional levels then for the EU as a whole. A more articulated and defined view on the post-2020 EU gas market should be an essential element of the EU's supply architecture regardless of whether gas stays in the fuel mix for the next two to three generations or whether it is used solely as a back-up fuel in case other generating technologies do not deliver.

The short-term vision

The short-term vision should equally cover three policy chapters: the Infrastructure Package implementation, the (expedited) implementation of the Third Energy Package, and the fine-tuning of the concept of solidarity. The implementation of these two Packages requires timely decision-making for full application since the window-of-opportunity for the cost-effective transition to a low carbon energy economy is anticipated to close around 2018. The long-term vision for the role of gas could be less meaningful if not supported by the short-term actions that are required. Short-term actions are therefore considered as the first step to moving beyond 2020. In addition, a further enhancement of the existing emergency mechanism would result in a strengthening of solidarity within the EU and, thus, contribute to global supply security.

The European Energy Infrastructure Package

New investments in long-haul and cross-border pipelines for gas are critical components of any supply Architecture. The Infrastructure Package covers a number of issues that call for timely implementation: enhancing the Project of Common Interest (PCI) process; streamlining the Cross-Border Cost-Benefit Analysis (CB-CBA) approach; expediting efficient CB-licensing and permitting; and specifying the role of public money versus private money. The three EU institutions should therefore work expeditiously on a decision on the Regulation, allowing it to enter into force as early as 2013. In addition, the various implementing devices, such as CBA-methodologies and arrangements for CB-regulatory decisions could start as soon as 2012 if prioritization by the Agency for the Cooperation of Energy Regulators (ACER) is allowed and facilitated.

The Third Energy Package

The Third Energy Package is a solid basis for organizing the EU gas market and the TSO industry. Implementation does not yet have the proper priority at the national level, which influences the work at EU-level. The process of establishing the Network Codes and the supporting Framework Guidelines should further facilitate a timely completion with some further political guidance, if necessary, by the Council. Refraining from addressing minutiae would streamline this process.

The ongoing cross-border restructuring process in the TSO-sector, which could be considered as a positive step towards further market integration, may require additional attention in order to manage an effective and supportive TSO-certification process. Once again, ACER plays an important preparatory role, especially when it comes to further strengthening the cooperation of National Regulatory Authorities (NRAs).

Securing regulatory stability to allow the necessary market dynamics deserves continued attention by all stakeholders and authorities. The ongoing Regional Gas Initiatives (RGI) and other informal discussion platforms have roles to play in seeking specific solutions for regionally specific issues. If these mechanisms are working effectively, an EU-wide model for an internal gas market would become less urgent.

High-level attention is needed and should be given to the two issues that are of significant concern to some of the EU's external suppliers. The relevant conditions in the Third Package, i.e. on non-EU ownership in infrastructures and on efficient cross-border transiting of gas flows, should be further articulated and discussed with external suppliers at the proper levels. These issues can, and should, be solved over the course of the next year or so.

The building of energy solidarity in the EU

The EU is on a promising path towards the building of EU energy solidarity both *ex ante*, when it comes to institution building for crisis prevention, and on the spot, in terms of crisis management in a spirit of solidarity.

Regulation (EU) No 994/2010 concerning measures to safeguard security of gas supply is the EU's key solidarity instrument providing a solid basis for the management of unforeseen supply interruptions on a short-term basis. Certain issues that still need to be resolved or are missing can be overcome based on the experiences from past crises. The transposition of the lessons learnt into the existing framework can further refine and improve the procedure in place.

Ultimately, the prerequisite to solidarity is transparency. In this respect the increased efforts in the area of foreign energy relations with supplier countries play an important role. Following the long awaited Communication of the EC in September 2011 here especially the proposal for a Decision setting up an information exchange mechanism with regard to intergovernmental agreements between Member States and third countries in the field of energy is a promising step in the right direction.

Appendix I

List of Participants at the FEEM, Clingendael and Loyola de Palcio Chair workshops that contributed to the debate (alphabetical order)

VAN AGT, Christof, NETHERLANDS
Senior Researcher at CIEP, Clingendael

AHNER, Nicole, ITALY
Coordinator of the Loyola de Palacio Chair, FSR, EUI

ASCARI, Sergio, ITALY
Gas Advisor, FSR, EUI

BIGANO, Andrea, ITALY
Senior Researcher, FEEM

BOLTZ, Walter, AUSTRIA
Executive Director E-control, Vice Chair Regulatory Board ACER

CARIELLO, Francesco, ITALY
Head of EU regulation, AEEG

CHECCHI, Arianna, ITALY
Analyst, Supply Market Intelligence, ENI

CLEUTINX, Christian, BELGIUM
Former Director General of the Euratom Supply Agency, and former Director at EC DG Energy, also in charge of EU-Russia dialogue, European Commission

COUPAYE, Noël, FRANCE
Head of European Affairs at the Infrastructures Division, GDF SUEZ

D'ALBERTI, Federico, ITALY
Regulatory, Environment and Innovation, Enel

DARBOUCHE, Hakim, UNITED KINGDOM
Research Fellow, Oxford Institute of Energy Studies (OIES)

DE GIOVANNI, Daniele, ITALY
EVP - Planning & Control and Business Development

DE JONG, Jacques, NETHERLANDS
Senior Fellow at CIEP, Clingendael

DE JONG, Dick, NETHERLANDS
Senior Fellow at CIEP, Clingendael

DE LA FLOR, Francisco, SPAIN
Regulatory Development Manager, Enagas

DESCHUYTENEER, Thierry, BELGIUM
Public Affairs Manager, Fluxys

FIP, Uwe, GERMANY
Senior Vice President, Eon Ruhrgas

FLOS, Antoni, SPAIN
Director of Corporate International Affairs, Gas Natural Fenosa

GARRUTO, Valentina, ITALY
Manager, Relations with International Authorities, ENI

GHILÈS, Francis, SPAIN
Senior Researcher at the Barcelona Center for International Affairs – CIDOB

GHEZI, Marco Luigi Giuseppe, ITALY
Long Term Market View and Supply Portfolio Development, ENI

GLACHANT, Jean-Michel, ITALY
Director, Florence School of Regulation, Holder of the Loyola de Palacio Chair on Energy, EUI

GOURAUD, Olivier, AZERBAIDJAN
Commercial Director, Total E&P

GRIGORIEV, Leonard, RUSSIA
Deputy Director General, Russian Energy Agency

GROENENDIJK, Wim, NETHERLANDS
Head International and Public Affairs, N.V. Nederlandse Gasunie

HAFNER, Manfred, ITALY
Fellow, Fondazione Eni Enrico Mattei (FEEM)

HALLACK, Michelle, ITALY
Jean Monnet Fellow, Loyola de Palacio Chair, EUI

HELD, Tanja, BELGIUM
Policy Officer, DG ENER, European Commission

JAHAN DE LESTANG, Martin, FRANCE
GDF SUEZ

KADERJAK, Peter, HUNGARY
Director of the Regional Centre for Energy Policy Research, Corvinus University of Budapest

KOVACS, Kristof, BELGIUM
EG ENER, European Commission

KRAMER, Marcel, SWITZERLAND
CEO, South Stream and former Chairman and CEO of Gasunie

LOCATELLI, Cathérine, FRANCE
Senior Researcher at CNRS and University of Grenoble

LORUBIO, Giuseppe, BELGIUM
Eurelectric – Union of the Electricity Industry

LE HÉNAF, Carol, FRANCE
Economist, GDF Suez

LOUDON, Margot, BELGIUM
Deputy Secretary General, Eurogas

MEULMAN, Leonie, NETHERLANDS
Researcher at CIEP, Clingendael

MITROVA, Tatiana, RUSSIA
Energy Research Institute of the Russian Academy of Sciences

MOSELLE, Boaz, UNITED KINGDOM
Managing Director at FTI Consulting

NORENG, Øystein, NORWAY
Professor, Oslo School of Management

PERCIVAL, Bas, NETHERLANDS
Researcher at CIEP, Clingendael

PIREDDA, Marco, ITALY
Head of Legislative Studies, ENI

POLS, Adri, NETHERLANDS
Commercial Manager Bergermeer Gas Storage at TAQA

PREINSTORFER, Dietmar, AUSTRIA
Head of International Relations, E-Control, Austria

RAKHOU, Erik, NETHERLANDS
NMA

ROBERTS, John, UNITED KINGDOM
Energy Security Specialist, Platts

ROCCHIO, Hannelore, ITALY
ESVP International Initiative Development Relations with Authorities and European Institutions, ENI

SAMMARCO, Giuseppe, ITALY
Executive Director, FEEM

SASS, Sebastian, SWITZERLAND
Head of EU and Regulatory Affairs, South Stream

SCHMITT VON SYDOW, Helmut, SWITZERLAND
Professor, University of Lausanne and European College Parma

SIKOW-MAGNY, Catharina, BELGIUM
Deputy Head of Unit Internal Market 1: Networks & Regional Initiatives, European Commission

SQUEGLIA, Claudia, ITALY
VP, Gas and Power and Non-Hydrocarbon Energy Market Scenarios and Long Term Strategic Options, ENI

SUND, Karen, NORWAY
Sundenergy

TAGLIAPIETRA, Simone, ITALY
Researcher, FEEM

TAVONI, Massimo, ITALY
Senior Researcher, FEEM

VAN DER LINDE, Coby, NETHERLANDS
Director CIEP, Clingendael

VAN HOOGSTRATEN, Jan Willem, NETHERLANDS
Managing Director Taqa Energy

VAN STIPHOUT, Mark, BELGIUM
DG Energy, European Commission

VANTAGGIATO, Francesca Pia, ITALY
Research Assistant, IERN, FSR, EUI

VAZQUEZ, Miguel, ITALY
Jean Monnet Fellow, Loyola de Palacio Chair on Energy, FSR, EUI

VINOIS, Jean-Arnold, BELGIUM
Acting Director, Security of Supply, Energy Markets and Networks, DG ENER, European Commission

VISSER, Martien, NETHERLANDS
Fellow at CIEP, Clingendael

VOßWINKEL, Jan S. , GERMANY
Head of Unit EU Energy Policy, CEP

WAGNER, Albrecht, AUSTRIA
WE & C

WESTGAARD, Geir, BELGIUM
Vice President, EU Affairs, Statoil ASA

WESTPHAL, Kirsten, GERMANY
Researcher, German Institute for International and Security Affairs

Appendix II

List of Speakers and Chair Persons of
WILTON PARK CONFERENCE 1121
Mon 23/01/2012 to Wed 25/01/2012
EU and UK gas security of supply

AL-MARRI, Rashid, QATAR
General Manager, South Hook Gas, London

BALDWIN, John, UNITED KINGDOM
Group Political Adviser, BP plc, London

BENSCHOP, Dick, NETHERLANDS
Vice President, Gas Market Development, Shell Nederland B.V., The Hague

BRABO, Torben, DENMARK
Market Director, Energinet, Ballerup

BURGE, Richard, UNITED KINGDOM
Chief Executive, Wilton Park, Steyning

BURGOS ALONSO, Cristobal, SPAIN
Adviser, Internal Energy Markets, European Commission, Brussels

CORBEAU, Anne-Sophie, FRANCE
Senior Gas Expert, International Energy Agency, Paris

DE JONG, Jacques, NETHERLANDS
Senior Fellow, Clingendael International Energy Programme, The Hague

GLACHANT, Jean-Michel, FRANCE
Director, Florence School of Regulation, Florence

GRANT, Robert, UNITED KINGDOM
Programme Director, Wilton Park, Steyning

GRIGORIEV, Leonid, RUSSIA
Deputy Director General, Russian Energy Agency, Ministry of Energy of the Russian Federation, Moscow

HAFNER, Manfred, ITALY
Fellow, Fondazione Eni Enrico Mattei (FEEM), Milan

HENDRY, Charles, UNITED KINGDOM
Minister of State, Department for Energy and Climate Change, London

HENRIKSEN, Per Rune, NORWAY
State Secretary, Norwegian Ministry of Petroleum and Energy, Oslo

HOSKER, Edmund, UNITED KINGDOM
Director, International, Europe and Energy Security, Department for Energy and Climate Change (DECC), London

LAIDLAW, Sam, UNITED KINGDOM
Chief Executive, Centrica plc, Windsor

LYLE, Colin, UNITED KINGDOM
Board Member and Gas Committee Chairman, European Federation of Energy Traders (EFET), Amsterdam

ORBAN, Anita, HUNGARY
Ambassador-at-Large for Energy Security, Ministry of Foreign Affairs, Budapest

PFLÜGER, Friedbert, GERMANY
Director European Centre for Energy and Resource Security (EUCERS), Kings College London, Berlin

RILEY, Alan, UNITED KINGDOM
Professor of Law, City Law School, City University, London

ROBERTS, John, UNITED KINGDOM
Energy Security Specialist, Platts, London

SCHMITT VON SYDOW, Helmut, GERMANY
Professor, University of Lausanne and European College Parma, Brussels

STEELE, Graeme, UNITED KINGDOM
European Policy and Interconnectors Manager, National Grid plc, Warwick

TAYLOR, Pamela, UNITED KINGDOM
Associate Partner, Ofgem, London